Dressing the Part

Dressing the Part
Sternberg, Dietrich, and Costume

Sybil DelGaudio

Rutherford ● Madison ● Teaneck
Fairleigh Dickinson University Press
London and Toronto: Associated University Presses

Associated University Presses
440 Forsgate Drive
Cranbury, NJ 08512

Associated University Presses
25 Sicilian Avenue
London WC1A 2QH, England

Associated University Presses
P.O. Box 338, Port Credit
Mississauga, Ontario
L5G, 4L8 Canada

The paper used in this publication meets the requirements
of the American National Standard for Permanence of Paper
for Printed Library Materials Z39.48-1984.

Library of Congress Cataloging-in-Publication Data

DelGaudio, Sybil, 1944–
  Dressing the part : Sternberg, Dietrich, and costume / Sybil
DelGaudio.
    p. cm.
  Includes bibliographical references and index.
  ISBN 0-8386-3471-0 (alk. paper)
  1. Von Sternberg, Josef, 1894–1969—Criticism and interpretation.
2. Costume. 3. Dietrich, Marlene. I. Title.
PN1998.3.V66D4 1993
791.43'0233'092—dc20   91-58953
                                                                CIP

PRINTED IN THE UNITED STATES OF AMERICA

For my mother,
who taught me to love movies

Contents

Acknowledgments   9

1. Introduction   13
2. A Developing Aesthetic: *The Salvation Hunters* and
   Underworld   23
3. Role-Playing and Performance as Layering: *The Blue
   Angel* and *Blonde Venus*   29
4. Deception, Spying, and Disguise: *Dishonored, Shanghai
   Express, The King Steps Out,* and *Jet Pilot*   63
5. Stylization as Distance: *Morocco* and *The Devil Is A
   Woman*   99
6. Sternberg vs. History: *The Scarlet Empress* and *I,
   Claudius*   127
7. The City as Cinema: *The Shanghai Gesture* and *Macao*   149
8. Self-Reflexive Films: *The Last Command* and *The Saga
   of Anatahan*   160

Notes   171
Bibliography   182
Index   191

Acknowledgments

While writing a book often seems a most lonely project, there are clearly many whose support made it less so.

I wish to thank the members of my defense committee at Columbia: Professor Raynor Crone of the art history department and Professor Richard Kuhns of the philosophy department, both of whom provided invaluable insight from related disciplines; Professor Stefan Sharff and Professor Andrew Sarris of the film department, both inspirational teachers throughout my many semesters in their classes, who helped me to formulate my own approach to cinema and made many important suggestions, backed by generous support, during my defense; and John Belton, my adviser, who read and reread my manuscript, and whose integrity as a scholar never allowed friendship to interfere with what was often tough, but always astute, objective criticism.

Several people helped me in screening some of the films I have written about, among them Stuart Linder of Films, Incorporated; the always-generous Bill Everson; and Charles Silver and Ron Magliozzi of the Museum of Modern Art Film Study Center.

Friends provided crucial support, the importance of which they are hardly ever conscious of. Liz Weis, her own work a model of fine scholarship and originality, encouraged me from the inception of my idea through its completion. Ellen Karsh's completion of her own dissertation under difficult conditions was inspirational, and her understanding of the Kaypro was essential to my recovery from computer-phobia. Patty Wineapple helped with tangibles such as xeroxing, but her real contributions were the intangibles of consistent support and faith.

Photographs are reproduced by courtesy of: The Museum of Modern Art/Film Stills Archive, Photofest, Movie Star News, and Jerry Ohlinger's Movie Material Store, Inc.

Dressing the Part

1

Introduction

For Hollywood, everything was larger than life, bigger than anything before or since. The diamonds were bigger, the furs were thicker; the silks, velvets, satins, chiffons were richer and silkier. There were miles of ostrich feathers, maribou, white fox, and sable; miles of bugle beads, diamanté and sequins. Hollywood was paved with glitter, shine and glory. Everything was an exaggeration of history, fiction and the whole wide extraordinary world.[1]

Beyond the early years of nameless players and morally identified clothing, Hollywood costume was inexorably linked to glamour, glitter and extravagance. Inseparable from the star system, which grew to enormous proportions in the 1930s, costume became the perfect vehicle for the display of Hollywood fantasy. If stars reflected the needs, dreams and drives of American society, their costumes were a palpable sign of wish fulfillment, displaying material success in a highly romanticized vision of fashion, fabric, accessory and trim.

Because of its association with the superficiality of image-making, the serious study of costume in film was initially limited to works which explored designs and designers as purveyors of Hollywood mystique and fantasy. Several of the early volumes have titles that express their rather specific viewpoints. *Those Glorious, Glamour Years,* by Margaret Bailey, *In a Glamorous Fashion* by Robert La-Vine, and *Hollywood Costume: Glamour! Glitter! Romance!* by Diana Vreeland and Dale McConathy all give attention to the luxury and sumptuousness of costume. Others either chronicle contributions of individual designers (*Costume Design In the Movies* by Elizabeth Leese) or examine the relationship between studio and product (*Hollywood Costume Design* by David Chierichetti). More recent serious study of costume has been done by such scholars as Charles Eckert, Maureen Turim and Jane Gaines,[2] among others, who have been primarily concerned with the intersection of Hollywood costume and the fashion industry. Very little work has been done on the way in which costumes signify within individual texts,

13

and there have been no attempts to study costume as a significant aspect of directorial style.[3]

Roland Barthes provides a means of looking at costume's signifying functions within individual texts by creating an ethic of costume through an analysis of the function of theatrical clothing.[4] Barthes's analysis suggests several areas in which costume can lose its "pure" function, threatening to smother the play with its own, independent values. In order to prevent such subordination of play to costume, a result which mars costume's functional role, costume must avoid what Barthes terms "diseases," or "errors." In addition to luxury or sumptuousness (a.k.a. glamour, in the language of Hollywood), which he identifies as the disease of money, Barthes categorizes the other diseases of costume as hypertrophies, or exaggerations, of its historical and aesthetic functions. The obsession with "archeological verism," which overdoes the historical function, and the excessive concern for a "formal beauty without relation to the play" are diseases which rob costume of its more important, intellectual function as an argument. They neglect the powerful semantic value by which costume can be read for its communication of ideas, information or sentiments.[5] It is the purpose of this study to investigate costume in film in terms of the way in which it functions as an argument or sign. Further, by looking at the way in which clothing functions narratively and thematically within the work of one director, Josef von Sternberg, the study will analyze the way in which such signs can be identified as an aspect of directorial style.

Film scholars have long identified directorial style through various elements of mise-en-scène. Camera movement in the films of Max Ophuls or Otto Preminger, deep focus photography in the films of William Wyler and Orson Welles, the sumptuous set decoration of a Lubitsch comedy—each aesthetic principle has developed into an identifying stylistic element. Costume, also an aspect of a film's mise-en-scène, has never been fully investigated as an element of directorial style. In addition, the collaborative effort of film's creative activities has focused responsibility for a film's costumes on the designer, producer or studio, ignoring the often essential contribution of the director in creating a pattern of narrative and thematic design communicated by elements of mise-en-scène. The following study of costume in the films of Josef von Sternberg attempts to investigate Barthes's notion of costume's primary function, that of sign, and to identify the way in which Sternberg's attention to costume-as-sign became an important element of that director's visual style, inseparable from the film's narrative or thematic design. By demonstrating that costume as an element of mise-en-scène is central to the study of Sternberg's work, I hope to suggest that research into costume signification in the work of other directors would be valuable as well.

Sternberg's own interest in clothing dates from his early days as an apprentice in a millinery shop,[6] a job which may, in part, explain his attention to costume in his films. Later, Sternberg was employed as a stock clerk in a lace house in New York, a position which introduced him to the material that would reappear so often in his films.[7]

Even in his personal manner of dress, Sternberg would costume himself as "the director." Imitating the style of his idol, Erich von Stroheim, Sternberg would appear on the set in a variety of outfits that signified directorial authority, and the riding breeches, beret and boots indicated his complete immersion in the role.[8] John Baxter reports that during the shooting of *I, Claudius*, Sternberg added a personally designed Javanese turban and a coat that was nearly too heavy to lift.[9] Sternberg's attention to his own clothing extended to a penchant for the details of other clothing. Edith Head reports that on the set the "Svengali director would spend hours choosing the right hat or handbag, or take pains to adjust a wisp of hair on [Dietrich's] cheek."[10]

Of course, the proof of Sternberg's obsession with costume as an element of mise-en-scène lies not in his autobiography, but in his films. From his first film, *The Salvation Hunters*, to his last, *The Saga of Anatahan*, Sternberg shows evidence of a developing aesthetic that utilized costume as an organizing principle for his films' narrative and thematic designs.

But while there is evidence of Sternberg's interest in costume throughout his work, the richest and most developed use of costume appears in the group of films he made in collaboration with Paramount, Marlene Dietrich and Travis Banton. The studio/star/designer/director team produced a series of films, beginning with *Morocco* in 1930 and ending with *The Devil Is A Woman* in 1935, that, because of the complex richness of the collaboration, gave Sternberg the atmosphere (through the studio), the vehicle (through the star), and the sense of design (through the designer) to develop a style in which costume figured crucially as an element of his film's narrative and thematic designs.

Paramount in the thirties was considered Hollywood's most "European" studio.[11] Many of Paramount's designers, technicians and craftsmen had come to Paramount from Germany, and their visually ornate films seemed clearly influenced by UFA, the German studio known for its expressionist style. With its "cinema of half-light and suggestion; witty, intelligent, faintly corrupt,"[12] Paramount produced films which proved to be stylistically well-suited to the visual clutter and baroque design of Sternberg's frames. B. P. Schulberg, Paramount production chief at the time of Sternberg's first film, *The Salvation Hunters*, was extremely supportive of the director. However, when Schulberg was replaced by Ernst Lubitsch in 1935, at a time when Sternberg's popularity with both critics and public was beginning to wane, the director's control became severely limited.

Equally as important as his association with Paramount was the fact that Sternberg worked during an era which encouraged his style. The thirties, known as the "golden era of cinema glamour," was a period in which films glorified the traditional American dream of success and riches, though the country was in the grip of the Great Depression. Margaret Bailey reports that it was a time when "reality mingled with fantasy, and the screen presented us with romanticized and idealized images of ourselves."[13] The star was the main object of Hollywood fantasy, and studios spent more effort and money creating their stars than they had ever done in the past, or would ever again do in the future.

Paramount's star was Dietrich, the slightly plump German woman who, redesigned by Sternberg, so conveniently followed his directions and orders. Their association, marked by a relationship which Sternberg would describe as that between master and servant,[14] permitted Sternberg the kind of control so crucial to his art. His effort to maintain this control extended to every aspect of planning and production, and led to a struggle between the director and the very nature of the medium in which he worked.

Before considering the essential character of Sternberg's work, it is important to understand his association with designer Travis Banton, Paramount's chief costume designer in the thirties. Banton had worked on *The Drag Net*, a 1928 Sternberg film, of which there is no known extant print, but his first Dietrich film was *Morocco*. (The earlier *The Blue Angel* had been designed by the Hungarian designer Varady, whom Sternberg chose for his erotic designs.)[15]

Banton was brought to Hollywood in 1924, when Paramount hired him to design the costumes for the high fashion film, *The Dressmaker from Paris*. He had been a fashion designer in New York and had achieved some fame as the creator of Mary Pickford's wedding gown. When Howard Greer left Paramount in 1927, Banton became the studio's chief designer.[16] While he worked with many female stars (Clara Bow, Claudette Colbert, Carole Lombard and Mae West, among others), his most successful association was with Dietrich. David Chierichetti asserts that Banton's contribution to the Sternberg/Dietrich films was as crucial in the formation of the

P1167-466

Travis Banton with Marlene Dietrich. (Photofest)

Dietrich image as that of Lee Garmes, the cinematographer whose lighting created the classic look of Dietrich's face.[17]

While Sternberg's association with the team of Paramount, Dietrich and Banton afforded him an opportunity to evolve a personal style which utilized clothing signification as an element of a film's narrative and thematic design, it also provided him with a collective forum in which to develop certain ideas about the representational nature of the cinematic image.

The identification of the basic elements of the medium by both the Bazinian realists and the Eisensteinian/Arnheimian formalists forms the foundation for the theoretical principles advanced by Jurij Lotman's semiotic/structural study of cinema. Lotman's theories, heavily influenced by Russian formalism (Shklovsky and Tynyanov), Mukarovsky in Czechoslovakia, Ivanov in Russia and Jakobson in the United States, seek to investigate cinema's own sign system while also approaching the same questions of cinematic essence investigated by Bazin, Kracauer and Arnheim, among others, to arrive at an understanding of the aesthetics of cinema.

Lotman's theories regarding the illusion of reality in cinema are useful in isolating Sternberg's exploration of cinema's binary nature. According to Lotman, photography, and consequently cinematography, has its own documentary reliability, but its very advantages need to be overcome, since the aim of art is not simply to render an object, but rather to make it a carrier of meaning. Automatic representation, then, had to be subjected to the laws of creativity. For Lotman, art requires a twofold experience: the viewer, in order to express genuinely artistic emotions, must be simultaneously aware and unaware of the artifice before him.

> The duality of perception of a work of art leads to the fact that the greater the similarity of direct resemblance of art and life, the more strongly, at the same time, must the audience feel the conventionality. . . . Almost forgetting that he is experiencing a work of art, the viewer or reader must never forget it completely. Art is a living phenomenon and dialectically contradictory.[18]

It is clear that, in isolation, neither Bazinian realism nor the formative theories of Arnheim satisfy Lotman's theoretical inquiries. His theory is based on the recognition and appreciation of both of these apparent polarities, and derives its artistic validity from the tension that constantly exists between them.

Thus the attempts of cinematography to merge completely with life and the desire to manifest its cinematographic specifics, the conventionality of its language, to assert the sovereignty of art within its own sphere—these are the enemies which are constantly in need of each other. Like the north and south poles of a magnet, they do not exist without each other and form that field of structural tension in which the real history of cinematography operates.[19]

It is this field of structural tension created by cinema's two poles ("life" vs. "art") that Sternberg constantly explores. While there is evidence of such exploration in all aspects of Sternberg's artistic process, from the assertion of control over casting, creation of the star, choice of scripts and other preproduction decisions, to his meticulous attention to details of mise-en-scène, this study will concentrate on the way in which costume signification expresses certain polarities within the cinema. Realized in the language of costume—i.e., masquerade, incongruity, disguise, role-playing, layering, exoticism, glamour and campy artifice—cinema's ability to both record and transform becomes a central concern of Sternberg's work. In her 1972 essay on Josef von Sternberg, Joyce Rheuben characterized the director's personal style as a constant display of tension between reason and emotion. She focuses specifically on contentions between discipline and indulgence, intellect and faith, civilization and savagery, and revelation and concealment. In regard to his style of revealing and concealing, she stresses, at one point, Sternberg's mise-en-scène: a clutter of compositional excess that includes veils, nets, gauze, smoke, shadow and other visual obstructions. As Rheuben suggests, in Sternberg's films there exists a "stylistic strategy to accommodate that inner tension between revealing and concealing his familiar preoccupations."[20]
As Sternberg himself stated:

> To reality, one should prefer the illusion of reality. Otherwise, you do what Jean Rouch did in *Jaguar* . . . you film everything that happens in front of the camera. This is documentary, it is not art.[21]

Throughout his career. Sternberg struggled to define his art in ways that would differentiate it from "documentary." Beginning with his first film, *The Salvation Hunters* in 1925, Sternberg creates a visual atmosphere, complemented by enigmatic characterization, that suggests his resistance to film's "documentary" tendency. Costume signs begin to become an important part of his struggle in *Underworld* and *The Last Command*. But even in the other pre-Dietrich films, *The Docks of New York* and *Thunderbolt* (there are no known extant prints of *The Exquisite Sinner, The Sea Gull, The*

Drag Net or *The Case of Lena Smith*), Sternberg attempts through
the use of light to limit the accessibility of the image *(The Docks
of New York)* or concentrates on themes of deception and secrecy
(Thunderbolt). The latter themes appear frequently throughout his
career and ultimately form the thematic basis for his resistance
strategy.

Throughout his career, Sternberg's struggle would not be restricted to the films themselves, but would also involve the power
structure of the Hollywood studio system, and his attempts to control every aspect of the creative process often diverted his energies.
Some of the films which he considered "only an assignment" reveal
evidence of the director's style, and I have dealt with those in greater
detail in their own, separate sections. *Jet Pilot* and *Macao*, for example, both produced by Howard Hughes, reveal many Sternbergian
touches. *An American Tragedy* was made while waiting for Dietrich
to return from Europe after they had completed *Dishonored*. *Crime
and Punishment* and *The King Steps Out* were part of a two-picture
contract with Columbia. *Sergeant Madden* was a fulfillment of a
contract with M-G-M that evolved as a result of an aborted effort
on a Hedy Lamarr picture begun by Sternberg and finished by Frank
Borzage.[22] All seem to indicate the absorption of Sternberg's artistic
struggles by the effort to resist studio interference. As his popularity
waned with critics and public, and as the projects grew more infrequent and less interesting, Sternberg waited for a chance to freely
exercise his artistic energies. Of the films he made after the Dietrich
cycle, his unfinished project, *I, Claudius, The Shanghai Gesture*, and
his last film *The Saga of Anatahan* provided the director with the
most freedom, the latter film having been made primarily as an attempt to assert complete control over every aspect of production.

But even in films which pay less attention to costume signs than
those of the Dietrich cycle, Sternberg was concerned with themes
and techniques that explored cinema's basic nature. *The Docks of
New York* is a film in which atmosphere is created and the image
obscured with light; *Thunderbolt*, Sternberg's first sound film, deals
with secrecy; and the two adaptations, *An American Tragedy* and
Crime and Punishment, are both concerned with deception. While
costume cannot be considered the organizing principle in any of
these films, each of them contains some references to costume as it
defines character *(The Docks of New York* and *Crime and Punishment)* or expresses theme *(An American Tragedy* and *Thunderbolt)*.

In the Dietrich cycle, Sternberg discovers his most fertile atmosphere for the exploration of costume signs, and each of the films of
this period is organized around a central theme which is developed

in terms of such signs. *The Blue Angel* deals with appearance and reality, and the performer as dissembler; *Morocco,* also about a performer, questions appearance and reality through campy artifice and incongruity; *Dishonored* deals with spying and deception; *Shanghai Express,* also about deception, presents characters who are in disguise; *Blonde Venus,* another film about a performer, deals with roleplaying; *The Scarlet Empress* gives Sternberg an opportunity to exercise his artistic will against the backdrop of history; and *The Devil Is A Woman* presents deception in the form of a classic and glamorous femme fatale. Later films deal with familiar themes. *Jet Pilot* is about deception and spying; *Macao* and *The Shanghai Gesture* deal also with deception, though the mystery and lies are connected with a fatal city rather than a fatal woman; and *I, Claudius,* his incomplete project, shows evidence of Sternberg's interest in history. The approach he uses is similar to that in *The Scarlet Empress. The Saga of Anatahan,* Sternberg's last film, deals with truth and illusion in a microcosm that represents the medium of cinema itself. It was a final attempt to exercise total control over his medium by creating a world which would serve as its metaphor.

In the following chapters I will analyze Sternberg's career-long fascination with such themes as deception, the interplay between both appearance and reality, display and concealment, and ambiguity and role-playing. I will show how they are characterized by costume signs such as disguise, masquerade, cross-dressing and costume gestures such as dressing, undressing, and striptease. The recurrence of these themes and motifs emphasize the continuity in Sternberg's oeuvre. I do not mean to imply that Sternberg's work is static. The relentlessness of his exploration of the properties of his medium represents, rather, a kind of dynamism that imparts an artistic vitality to each of Sternberg's films. While his thematic concerns remain similar, his stylistic methods differ in accordance with the studio/ director power structure of each individual effort. For this reason, I have not chosen a strictly chronological treatment of the films, though the chapters do fall into a general chronological progression. Chapter 2 covers Sternberg's silent period. It deals specifically with the films (*The Salvation Hunters* and *Underworld*) which appear to represent a developing aesthetic in terms of themes and style and shows how they are related to clothing signification. Chapter 3 looks at Sternberg's films about role-playing (*The Blue Angel* and *Blonde Venus*). They investigate elements of cinema and form patterns of concern that find their most complete fulfillment in Sternberg's last and most clearly self-reflexive film, *The Saga of Anatahan.* Chapter 4 examines Sternberg's interest in deception and/or spying and their appropriate sartorial signifier, disguise. It discusses *Dishonored, Shanghai Express, Jet Pilot* and *The King Steps Out.* Chapter 5 describes a change in Sternberg's approach to costume. It analyzes his use of stylization as a distancing device in *Morocco,* which distances through campy artifice, and *The Devil Is A Woman,* which distances through glamour and characterization. Chapter 6 investigates Sternberg's method of approaching history, analyzing his resistance to its "reality" in *The Scarlet Empress* and the unfinished *I, Claudius.* Chapter 7 suggests a relocation of Sternberg's self-reflexivity—a substitution of the city for the star in *Macao* and *The Shanghai Gesture.* Chapter 8 deals with Sternberg's self-reflexive films, *The Last Command* and *The Saga of Anatahan.*

Throughout this study, I have attempted to examine both the consistencies and the changes in Sternberg's work, while always considering the working conditions that affected Sternberg's directorial control. As we shall see, throughout a career that was marked by artistic struggle and commercial success and failure, Sternberg's style developed a remarkable consistency in its very nature. Even in periods of greatest difficulty for him, Sternberg never gave up his interest in the nature of cinema, an interest that informed the creation of what became known as Sternbergian style.

2

A Developing Aesthetic: *The Salvation Hunters* and *Underworld*

Sternberg's first film, *The Salvation Hunters* (1925), and the later silent effort, *Underworld* (1927), afford a look at the fledgling director's early attempts to approach his medium, and contain adumbrations of the high Sternbergian style of the 1930s.

The Salvation Hunters, a heavily symbolic film, deals with the lives of three characters—the Boy, the Girl and the Child—who, as victims of Fate and "humans who crawl close to the earth," attempt to escape their environment and move towards a better life, symbolized by the sun. Like Sternberg's typically cluttered later mise-en-scènes, the setting contains various nets and ropes, signs of the waterfront. The strongest image, however, is that of a relentless dredge, which constantly cuts across the frame; its presence serves to emphasize faith in the potential for change. Sternberg's frames are often decidedly pictorial, i.e., static, and the kinetic nature of the medium, here represented by the movement of the dredge, suggests an early challenge to this static quality. Pictorialization, a method Sternberg develops more fully later in his work through lighting, frame clutter and visual density, becomes a sign of his artistic will. Sternberg's iconography is a kind of graphic immobility which is opposed in this film by the constant movement of the dredge, an opposition of movement and stasis to which Sternberg would later return in *The Scarlet Empress.* An early sign of Sternberg's attention to costume emerges in the intertitle's description of a woman "who has fallen as low as her stockings," while the central characters are clothed in costumes emblematic of the types they represent. Boy, Girl and Child wear the simple, universal clothing of the poor working class (the Boy is dressed in jeans and a shirt; the Girl wears a plain, unfashionable dress; the Child is dressed in overalls which he has outgrown), while more affluent pimps and johns dress in dapper suits. There is even a Sternberg look-alike: the Gentleman who generously offers money to the needy Girl without asking for anything

Boy, Girl, Child, and other characters from *The Salvation Hunters*. (Museum of Modern Art Film Stills Archive)

in return. He is a forerunner of later Sternberg analogues such as the humane Adolph Menjou in *Morocco* and the understanding William Powell in *The Last Command*.

The enigmatic nature of this film's characters reflects, in part, Sternberg's resistance to the cinema's representational transparency. Andrew Sarris calls *The Salvation Hunters* a modernist film, since it indicates Sternberg's reluctance to be explicit in regard to his characters. Sarris says Sternberg's reluctance is shown on the visual level through his consistent use of veils and filters. Dramatically, Sternberg avoids situations in which characters can explain their motivations, thus always retaining a degree of mystery.[1]

While Sternberg's work in this area does not fully develop until he finds a suitable cinematic forum in the richly conceived costume signs of the Dietrich cycle, there is evidence in *The Salvation Hunters*, as well as in two of his other silent efforts (*Underworld* and *The Last Command*) of a developing aesthetic.

Underworld (1927) is noteworthy in Sternberg's developing oeuvre for three major reasons. Firstly, it is the earliest Sternberg film to pay significant attention to costume signs. Secondly, it is the first of several Sternberg films to utilize the metaphor of the ball, or carnival, as a symbol of illusion. Thirdly, it presents ideas concerning perception, misperception and deception that pervade Sternberg's later work and find their most complete fulfillment in costume signs.

Based on a story by Ben Hecht, *Underworld* concerns a Chicago gangster named Bull Weed (George Bancroft) who employs and befriends an alcoholic lawyer with the unlikely name of Rolls Royce (Clive Brook). Weed ultimately loses his girlfriend, "Feathers" McCoy (Evelyn Brent), to Rolls following his (Weed's) imprisonment for the murder of another gangster, who had tried to sexually attack his moll.

The story as Sternberg approached it became, according to Marcel Oms, less a gangster story than a "description of humanity at its different levels."[2] The complex characterizations, coupled with the absence of generic signs of the gangster picture, support such a view.

"Feathers" McCoy, so nicknamed because of her taste in clothing, is the character who best exemplifies Sternberg's early attention to the emblematic potential of costume. Sternberg himself referred to his participation in Brent's costuming:

> One of the actresses assigned to me I named Feathers, and to justify this I covered her with feathers, and even had feathers sewn on her underwear. Perhaps she felt uncomfortable in the tickling garment, for at one time while I told her how to act, she threw a shoe at me.[3]

While the above statement sounds more like Stroheimian obsession than Sternbergian symbolism, Brent's reaction was more likely provoked by emotional exasperation than by physical discomfort, since Sternberg was not, as this study shall reveal, interested in realism, except insofar as it presented him with a convenient backdrop against which to exercise his artistic will. A further contrast between Stroheim and Sternberg is pointed out by Peter Baxter, who suggests that while the films of both may have dealt with the "lower depths of society" (i.e., prostitutes, show people, etc.), Stroheim stripped them to their corrupt souls while Sternberg "heaped them with glamour until they became unrecognizable."[4]

In fact, Sternberg's "glamourizing" with accessories may have been the result of his apprenticeship in a millinery shop. The trimmings which became part of his visual style were those most frequently used in the millinery trade, i.e., fur, veils and feathers. Edith

Evelyn Brent as Feathers McCoy in *Underworld*. (Photofest)

Head suggests that glamour didn't really enter the picture until the Dietrich/Banton team was formed. Their collaboration created the "exotic, super high-fashion look" (characterized by feathers, veils and other glamorous accessories) that required Banton to create it and Dietrich to pull it off.[5]

But while Brent did not possess the potential for glamour that Dietrich had, her costumes in *Underworld* suggest Sternberg's early concern with eroticism/exoticism conveyed by costume accessory and gesture. Brent is introduced in a scene which Sternberg would repeat in his introduction of Dietrich in *Dishonored*. As she enters the Dreamland Cafe, the gangster hangout in *Underworld*, she immediately adjusts her stockings. The gesture is erotically charged, even though, in maintaining its long shot position, the camera refuses to fetishize her leg through close-up. As she adjusts her makeup, one of her feathers floats through the air and down the stairs to the lower level, where Rolls is sweeping the floor. The downy missile lands in his hand. In addition to providing a visual transition fatally linking these two characters, the feather also serves to suggest their erotic connection. Later in the film it is a feather left behind after an assignation between Feathers and Rolls, that finally betrays the lovers.

John Baxter has pointed out Sternberg's attention to bird symbolism, noting that birds figure significantly throughout Sternberg's work. Baxter suggests that birds enrich Sternberg's films with religious, sexual and psychological symbolism, providing each work with poetic significance.[6] In *Underworld*, Brent's character name and her costume emphasize her influence over the actions of the men in the film, and the feathers she leaves in her path suggest her omnipotence: It is Feathers who seduces Rolls Royce, a seduction that begins with the aforementioned floating feather. (It is also the telltale mark of deception, since as previously mentioned, it is a feather discovered in Rolls' cigarette case that informs Bull that his trust in his two friends has been violated.)

Actually, Feathers' omnipotence extends beyond her individual costumes. At the gangsters' annual ball, referred to in a title card as "a devil's carnival," Sternberg introduces a setting to which he will return in *Dishonored* and *The Devil Is A Woman*. While the ball in *Underworld* is not a literal masquerade, as it is in the later films, it is, with its cluttered visuals (confetti streamers, partying people and general visual chaos), symbolically a masquerade that functions as a favorite Sternbergian sign of concealment and deception. The growing passion between Rolls Royce and Feathers is a feeling that the characters are trying to conceal, if not altogether resist. Even the motivation for the ball, referred to as "the underworld's annual armistice," seems a weak effort to bridge the insurmountable gap between rival gangsters, and the notion of an armistice between them is a deception in itself. Marcel Oms has commented on Sternberg's use of the carnival, or festival, as a sign of sensory delirium by which men disguise the truth of their painful emotions.[7] Indeed, Sternberg's festival abounds with signs of such delirium: the drunkenness, the emotional outbursts, the wildly chaotic mise-en-scène, the montage of hysterical faces.

Visually, Sternberg creates a transition which links the feathers of Brent's costume to the confetti streamers of the carnival rooms. Buck Mulligan's girlfriend wears a costume which combines the look of feathers with the look of confetti (a black dress trimmed with streamers). The costume serves as the overpowering visual sign of clutter and concealment in this mad world of deception and illusion. The confetti streamers closely resemble Brent's feathers, and they clutter the frame (emphasizing her ubiquity) with signs of molting. At one point, confetti covers a statue of a bull—a symbol of Feathers' dominance over Bull—as the latter lies stone-cold drunk on the floor, covered, as well, with the paper streamers.

If clothes make the man (as they have with the transformed and dapper Rolls Royce, outfitted by Bull after being hired by him), then they surely unmake the woman, as Feathers' feathers betray her emotional infidelity. The telltale feathers also lead to a misperception on Bull's part. He assumes that the relationship between Rolls and Feathers means that their promised plan to help him escape is merely a deception. In fact, the two, plagued by their loyalty to him and a desire to remain decent, cannot betray Bull. When Bull escapes from prison to avenge their "disloyalty," he discovers his error and even helps the lovers escape, saying he learned a lesson that was "worth more to [him] than [his] whole life." Here, as Eileen Bowser suggests, the recognition of the strength of the love that exists between Feathers and Rolls supersedes his own needs, while the recognition of their loyalty provides Bull with a means of redemption.[8] While the costume signs in *Underworld* do not approach the richness of those developed throughout the Dietrich cycle, the importance of their use in *Underworld* should not be minimized. The film introduces questions of deception and loyalty, perception and misperception, which will develop into the major thematic concerns of Sternberg's oeuvre, while presenting the director's first real attempts to visualize those concerns in terms of costume signs.

3

Role-Playing and Performance as Layering:
The Blue Angel and *Blonde Venus*

In *The Blue Angel* and in *Blonde Venus,* Sternberg begins to develop a strategy for controlling his medium by creating a complex structural system of layering, both informational and visual, to maintain inaccessibility, and, in Peter Wollen's terms, to break the existential bond between cinema and the real world, between fact and image.[1]

Wollen identifies Sternberg's resistance strategy as one which primarily stresses the pictorial nature of cinema through the creation of his own stylistic, painterly interpretation of reality. Wollen distinguishes Sternberg's style from that of Roberto Rossellini.

> The contrast to Rossellini is striking. Rossellini preferred to shoot on location; Von Sternberg always used a set. Rossellini avers that he never uses a shooting script and never knows how a film will end when he begins it; Von Sternberg cut every sequence in his head before shooting it and never hesitated while editing. Rossellini's films have a rough-and-ready, sketch-like look; Von Sternberg evidently paid meticulous attention to every detail. Rossellini uses amateur actors, without makeup; Von Sternberg took the star system to its ultimate limit with Marlene Dietrich and revelled in hieratic masks and costumes.[2]

This chapter will explore Sternberg's interpretation of nature, as well as Lotman's notions of cinematic tensions between life and art through an analysis of the way in which costume works. Both *The Blue Angel* and *Blonde Venus* are examples of Sternberg films that use costume signs to suggest resemblance to the natural world while simultaneously foregrounding difference.

Based on Heinrich Mann's 1909 novel, *Professor Unrat, The Blue Angel* is the story of the rigid, bourgeois Professor Rath, who, in attempting to prevent the moral ruination of his students by the cabaret performer Lola-Lola, himself falls victim to her irresistible charms, marries her, loses his respected position at the local high school, and proceeds to live a life of humiliation, finally ending in ignominy and death.

The Blue Angel, Sternberg's first collaboration with Marlene Dietrich, marked the beginning of an association that was to continue throughout six years and seven films. Interestingly, the film serves, both narratively and stylistically, as a demonstration to cinemagoers who allow themselves to fall victim to temptations of the kind that destroy the ill-fated Professor Rath. For in creating his star, a process which developed throughout the seven Dietrich films, Sternberg played with the relationship between audience and idol. The object of desire (Dietrich) remains as inaccessible to the viewer as the reality of Lola-Lola remains to Professor Rath (Emil Jannings), and the film presents, in its specific narrative/thematic context, not only the temptation but its consequences. In a stunning display of directorial arrogance, Sternberg has emphasized the inaccessibility of the star while continuing to present her as the object of desire, and it is this game of hide-and-seek, the play with promise and denial, that fascinates Sternberg throughout his career.

The film's first scene stresses the theme of accessibility/inaccessibility explored throughout *The Blue Angel*. Following the credits, the film opens with a morning street scene and images of preparation for a market. A scrubwoman lifts an iron grill that covers a tobacco shop's glass door; on the door is a cabaret poster of the provocatively posed Lola-Lola. It is a gesture of theatrical introduction, a metaphorical raising of the curtain, a sign of promised revelation. It explores notions of the erotic while it introduces, not the star herself, but a photographic likeness of the star, much like the film image, which remains out of reach. The scrubwoman hurls her bucket of water at the poster, but because it has been stuck to the inside of the glass, it remains untouched. In this scene, Sternberg has explored cinema's pictorial essence, emphasizing its inaccessibility: just as the poster is made untouchable because of the invisible glass barrier, so is the reality of the star/performer kept at a distance by the real nature of the film image. While the film image seems to promise accessibility through its resemblance to the natural world, Sternberg's strategy is to stress its true otherness by maintaining and emphasizing its distance. As the scrubwoman begins to wipe the glass, she pauses to examine Lola-Lola's pose. Her clumsy, failed attempt to imitate the seductive posture suggests its exclusivity: this is not Everywoman, but Lola-Lola; this is not Everystar, but Dietrich. And it is her specialness, her uniqueness so meticulously created by Sternberg, that we are reminded of here.

Before discussing the way in which Sternberg utilizes costume to extend the metaphor of film's essential accessibility/inaccessibility, it may be useful to explore his efforts to create a star, who, on the surface, resembled woman, but as representative of the cinemato-graphic image and in her characterization, remained always inaccessible. Through the image of Dietrich and through his creation of her star persona, Sternberg maintains the tension between the reality of desire and the impossibility of its fulfillment.

The stimulation of desire, through presentation of the star in erotic positions, encourages the viewer to repress the knowledge that he/she is experiencing a work of art, while the impossibility of fulfillment (through the inaccessibility of character within the narrative, through charismatic apotheosizing of the star) prevents the viewer from forgetting it completely. Thus, Sternberg is constantly exploring that field of structural tension between the special "reality" of the cinematographic image and the desire to "assert the sovereignty of art within its own sphere."[3]

Sternberg saw his relationship to actors as similar to that between a ventriloquist and his dummy,[4] and it is this conception that he applied to his creation of Dietrich as star. The well-known Svengali/Trilby relationship is, as Sternberg himself described it, interesting in the way in which it permitted Sternberg to exercise complete control over the image of his star, presenting her as simultaneously accessible and inaccessible. By making Dietrich the object of desire through careful alteration of her physical self and meticulous presentation of her film image (carefully controlled lighting, close-ups, costumes, makeup, etc.), while simultaneously presenting her as the femme fatale by maintaining her inaccessibility through costume metaphors such as disguise, masquerade, etc., and the mediation of her performance, Sternberg made Dietrich the perfect vehicle for his exploration of cinema.

In discussing his creation of the Dietrich persona, and in a rare display of modesty, Sternberg attributes Dietrich's charms to the actress herself, while also revealing his strategy for concealment:

> I did not endow her with a personality that was not her own; one sees what one wants to see, and I gave her nothing that she did not already have. What I did was to dramatize her attributes and make them visible for all to see; though, as there were perhaps too many, I concealed some.[5]

Sternberg's fascination with a Cambodian myth about a turbulent ocean agitated for a thousand years that finally brought to its surface a woman who was to charm the world, indicates his obsession with the creation of his star from the turbulent ocean of 1929 Berlin. In

Sternberg's search for the perfect Lola-Lola, a visual representation of Heinrich Mann's "amoral woman whose flesh brought about the downfall of a high school professor,"[6] the director visualized a figure not unlike those painted by Belgian artist Felicien Rops, whose androgynous women Sternberg was familiar with.[7]

Rops, a symbolist whose work was colored with eroticism and satanism, often associated the idea of death with the female sex,[8] and John Baxter notes the similarities between Rops's etchings of young, nearly naked women in black stockings and male hats, and Lola's cabaret costume. Rops was also fond of using salacious cherubs to surround his women, and such elements of decor are also present in *The Blue Angel* in the advertising poster of Lola-Lola's cabaret act as well as in the stage decorations[9] and clock figures which complement her performance. Rops's cherubs appear in the film as the students who constantly hover around Lola, forming a coterie of youthful admirers.

Rops's association of woman with danger and his depiction of her sexual power was undoubtedly responsible for Sternberg's attraction to the artist's work. This attraction finds its most complete fulfillment in *The Devil Is A Woman,* but, as Andrew Sarris has pointed out, it pervades all of Sternberg's films.[10]

It was Dietrich's "cool indifference" that Sternberg was most drawn to, an indifference which appealed to his attraction to film's duality: accessible yet inaccessible, available yet elusive. Dietrich would become for Sternberg the human embodiment of cinematic essence and a means to that essence through the layering of star and character. As Frank McConnell has suggested in his analysis of *The Blue Angel*'s opening scene:

> If Lola-Lola lies behind the shield of glass . . . Dietrich lies behind the role of "Lola" even more inaccessibly and tantalizingly.[11]

Layering as distancing is also manifested in Sternberg's attraction to the performer as character. In *The Blue Angel,* and in *Morocco* and *Blonde Venus* as well, Dietrich's character is that of a performer, a kind of dissembler who acts as a middle-woman between character and star. Sternberg's performers are usually singers, women who spend a good deal of time in dressing rooms, readying themselves for the taking on of another role, the performance within the performance. The dual performance serves as another form of literal layering, and a strategy which maintains distance through obscurity.

The layering of the dual performance is furthered by the use of costume, and in the case of the intrafilmic performer, it may be useful to distinguish between costume worn by a character in or out of intrafilmic performance. As a visual representation of the intrafilmic performance, costume serves as another informational layer that maintains inaccessibility.

Inaccessibility through layering is exploited not only in the construction of each individual layer of the total performance (i.e., woman-as-star/woman-as-character), but also in Sternberg's photographing of his performer. Alexander Walker reports that Gunter Rittau, the cinematographer of *The Blue Angel,* used a special lens that had been given to him by Charles Rosher (who had been the cinematographer for many of Mary Pickford's films). Known as a "Rosher bullseye," the lens had the capability of duplicating human vision by seeming to couple concentration on details directly before it, with only a vague awareness of surrounding information. The result was a clear delineation of Dietrich's main features, combined with a soft-focus look to the rest of her face. The resulting visual image embodied the Dietrich enigma and highlighted the film's polarities.[12]

In addition to the layering of woman-as-star/woman-as-character and photographic technique, Sternberg exploited costume in a strategy which tantalized with the promise of display, while it simultaneously or alternately masked in an effort to conceal. As Walker suggests, "in matters of eroticism, [Sternberg] is the great coverer-up."[13]

Following the scene that introduces Professor Rath, Sternberg returns to the idea advanced by the first scene, i.e., the emphasis on the separation of the body of Lola-Lola from our experience of her by the invisible barrier of the film image. As Rath's students pass around photos of the beautiful Lola-Lola, we are reminded of her earlier representation in the poster. Here, however, Sternberg draws us teasingly closer to potential accessibility. In the photograph, Lola-Lola wears a tutu made of real feathers, and the boys salaciously attempt to blow it up so that they can see what she is or isn't wearing underneath. Here, Sternberg has brought us a step closer to Lola-Lola the performer by making greater our erotic experience of her. We are no longer separated from the representational likeness of Lola by a piece of glass, yet the experience is still not immediate due to the mediation of the photograph, and we are not permitted to experience the actual presence of Lola-Lola until the next scene, when she is shown in performance. Performance, however, as suggested above is still another layer which adds to mystery, increasing density and preventing accessibility. From the photographs of the previous scene, there is a fade-out to Lola's performance, where she is dressed in a cabaret outfit, with stockings and garters, a sequined bodice and a hair ribbon, a costume that delivers some of what the photograph held back. In one shot, Sternberg sectionalizes Lola's form by shooting her only from the waist down, fetishizing her legs. We have been moved another step closer to the character/star; however, we are still kept at a distance by the presentation of her in performance.

Following her introduction on stage, Lola is shown next in her dressing room, surrounded by the students who previously had had only limited access through photographs and performance. Here Lola prepares for the next performance, and her costume is a remarkable example of the use of costume as metaphor to express the contradiction between appearance and reality. Lola wears the eighteenth century costume of the French upper class, a costume whose details connoted "rigidity, dignity and seriousness."[14] Characteristic of this costume were the paniers, hoop-like devices that widened the skirt by means of whalebone. It is a costume that, historically, revealed very little, but which Sternberg alters significantly. When Lola turns her back to the audience, the costume is revealed as backless, and her buttocks and legs are on display to both the cabaret audience and the film audience. In addition, when light hits the paniers, they become translucent, thus not affording the protection from view or the maintenance of dignity supplied by the original historical costume. Sternberg's use of costume here explores the display/disguise function of dress investigated by art historian Anne Hollander, who suggests that clothing as disguise has a history, not only in Romantic literature, but in metaphor and allegory as well.[15] Hollander's notions of disguise, hide-and-seek, concealment and distraction serve to effectively summarize some of Sternberg's major strategies in the utilization of costume as sign or metaphor. However, Sternberg's ends go a step beyond the erotic function served by these costumes. As Andrew Sarris has observed, it is not merely through costume metaphor, but through plot as well, that Sternberg examines the nature of his medium, constantly investigating illusion and delusion through relationships between men and women and through issues of appearance and reality.[16]

When Lola leaves the stage and discovers the angry but smitten Professor Rath in her dressing room, she reminds him to maintain his dignity by removing his hat. The irony here will be made more apparent by a contrast which involves costume gestures: costume removal can signify dignity (as in the gentlemanly gesture of the removal of the hat) or indignity (as in the ensuing removal of undergarments). Moments later, Lola ascends the spiral stairs to her bedroom, and, removing her underpants, lets them fall on the face and shoulder of the disconcerted professor. Later, when a student discovers the underpants on the dressing room floor, he stuffs them into Rath's coat pocket. Rath removes them after he has arrived home, and thinking they are a handkerchief, wipes his face with them. The erotic chain of events has now been completed, and Sternberg has inched us closer to the physical reality of Lola through connection with a fetishized object that takes her place.

This theme of delusion by surface appearances, of mirage which promises more than it delivers, continues to be expressed throughout *The Blue Angel* in a variety of costume signs. While dressing in various costumes allows the performer to play a variety of roles, the removal of costume lends erotic force to the presentation of the nude or seminude body. Sternberg undoubtedly understood the erotic charge of both dressing and undressing, and commented on the carnal appeal of both gestures in theatrical performance.[17]

Undressing, a ritual that occurs frequently in Lola's dressing room, can be viewed as a highly charged message of erotic tease to both characters and audience. The casting off of garments implies a promise that is essentially undelivered by Lola. In fact, it is interesting to note that often Lola removes clothing as far as her undergarments, and undergarments, always the last item of clothing to be removed as well as the first item of clothing to be put on, are erotically charged. They are proximate to total nudity, but also serve as a protective stop sign in the maintenance of inaccessibility.

Undergarments, specifically underpants, were, until 1850, worn only by men—women wore underskirts and stockings gartered around the knee. Female performers always wore underpants while performing, but, according to Anne Hollander, such garments probably strengthened the association in the public's mind between the stage and sexual depravity by hinting at transvestism and the sexually forbidden.[18]

The frequent costume gestures that relate to underpants—i.e., their removal, their display, their mistaken identity by Rath—act as introduction to the notion of transvestism, or cross-dressing, a theme only hinted at in *The Blue Angel,* but expanded upon in later films (*Morocco* and *Blonde Venus* in particular). Here, there are suggestions of androgyny in the sexual crossover between Lola and the professor, and ultimately in Rath's emasculation by his wife, a process characterized by signs of androgyny throughout. His absorption into Lola's act, his playing of the fool in clown's costume, his servility to Lola as he helps her on with her stockings, all suggest the theme of sexual crossover so pervasive in Sternberg's work.

Lola's final rendition of "Falling in Love Again," in contrast to the first, more playful rendition, augments the idea of sexual crossover in its shift in attitude, posture and costume. Here she is far more androgynous, as she takes a characteristically masculine, defiant pose with legs spread across a chair turned backwards. This pose is in contrast to that in her earlier rendition, when, leaning back and grabbing her knee, she appears to be more offering, more openly seductive. In the second rendition, her costume is a more traditional vamp-like outfit (all black, tight-fitting sequined bodice, with stockings, garters and black hat) and her demeanor signals her change of character. Andrew Sarris has suggested that the change represents a psychological development in Dietrich's Lola from mere sensual passivity to a more forceful fatalism about the nature of her desires,[19] a change heightened by further crossover. For if, as Sarris indicates, "the professor has been defeated by Lola's beauty, Lola has been ennobled by the professor's jealousy,"[20] and in rejecting his initially accepted subservience, she has become more aware of her own desire.

"Ambivalent clothing"[21] is a term used by J. C. Flugel to describe the role played by clothes that both reveal and conceal, thus enhancing sexual stimulation. With Lola this ambivalence is most evident in her traditional cabaret costume: the tight-fitting bodice, garters and stockings, which permit an exposure of her legs. Lola's offer and withdrawal of sexual promise to Rath is presented through a costume metaphor which signifies their ensuing marriage. Lawrence Langner has characterized ambivalent clothing as a useful invention for the practical purposes of love and marriage:

> By revealing a certain amount of the body, much may be promised. By hiding even more, the wearer's ability to come up to expectations cannot be challenged. The more the body is covered, the greater can be the promise, and sometimes the less the performance.[22]

Lola's costume, therefore, is a foreshadowing of the failure of Rath's erotic expectations and Lola's withholding of the complete satisfaction of desire. The "promise" is further highlighted in the wedding reception scene in which Lola wears a traditional bridal gown, symbol of the supposed purity of the bride and a promise to hold the marriage vows sacred.[23] Specifically, Lola's cabaret costume derives some of its erotic power from the exposure of garments that are usually concealed. The black stockings and garters worn here as outer garments are "suggestive signposts to the lingerie above,"[24] or intensely associated with undefended nudity higher up,[25] further peaking masculine interest. In addition, the black stockings, also worn by the chorines who surround the star, are similar to those in cancan performances and in Toulouse-Lautrec posters, and harken back to the film's first image of the inaccessible, black-stockinged Lola on the advertising poster.

The much-publicized and celebrated Dietrich legs, quite on show in *The Blue Angel,* stimulated an angry response from Heinrich Mann, author of the novel on which the film was based. He declared that the success of the film would rely heavily "on the naked thighs of Miss Dietrich."[26] In fact, Dietrich's legs became more a matter of studio promotion than of camera attention, since her legs are often specifically concealed in later films; but their role as a fetish in *The Blue Angel* exploited the historical association of costume with the nude leg, as well as the voyeuristic impulse central in Sternberg's conception of male-female relationships. As Anne Hollander reports, voyeurism was as much encouraged by fashion history as by human psychology. Since women did not wear underpants, the nude leg was associated with more nudity above, thus explaining the masculine erotic preoccupation with being able to see up a woman's skirt.[27]

Besides the exposure of legs in Lola's cabaret performance, Sternberg brings the voyeuristic experience closer to the susceptible professor. When Rath bends over to retrieve cigarettes that have fallen under her dressing table, he comes face-to-leg with Lola's exposed limbs. Though unnerved, the professor lingers awhile in erotic contemplation. His response is, perhaps, not unlike the audience's: as Lola has come down from the stage to become a physical reality previously kept at a distance, so Dietrich, through Sternberg's camera close-ups, has bridged the distance between audience and star/character—through the removal of several layers—to arrive at a proximity which more intensely stimulates erotic desire. Alan Casty has noted the result of the highlighting of Dietrich's legs:

> Von Sternberg's images of Marlene Dietrich's legs (sexual and suggestive beyond the more explicit display of female flesh in later films) are perfect examples of his intricate and meaningful use of the stimuli of physical surface . . . Dietrich's legs insist on a physical frankness beyond their decadently artificial surroundings.[28]

Here again, Sternberg has returned to the concept of layering (and the removal of layers) to highlight the duality of erotic stimulation and response. As the cabaret audience and Professor Rath respond to the exposure of Lola's legs, so the film audience responds to the corporeal reality of Dietrich's legs and the degree of stimulation is once more under Sternberg's control.

While Sternberg was most attentive to the creation and presentation of his star, the costumes of other characters are also significant in the film's narrative and thematic design. Professor Rath's costumes, for example, chronicle his character deterioration from being a man of self-control and reason to being a fool whose erupting passions ultimately destroy him.

Rath is initially presented in the respectable garb of a teacher: suit and tie, later augmented by greatcoat and hat when he travels outdoors. The major change occurs after four years of marriage to Lola. Rath appears before a mirror, putting on makeup to become the clown in the cabaret's magic act. It is a transformation which has been frequently foreshadowed by the recurring figure of the clown whose place Rath has taken. Always present at times of Rath's loss of control regarding Lola, the clown serves as a sign of Rath's descent from restraint to passion, from respected professional to object of ridicule. Rath's transformation is again foreshadowed in the wedding reception scene, in which Lola, clucking like a hen, encourages Rath to crow like a rooster. Later, his crowing is incorporated into his act as a painful manifestation of his cuckolding and his emasculation. The rooster and the fool, both symbols of the victimization of man by the unfaithful woman, have been incorporated into Rath's clown and his humiliation is completed by his forced appearance at a return engagement in his hometown. Rath has actually been shamed into an appearance at the Blue Angel nightclub by Kiepert, the company manager and magician, who reminds him that he has been supported by Lola for four years and owes her some reciprocity. Noteworthy in this scene is Lola's domestic costume: she wears an apron and her hausfrau-like appearance ironically highlights Rath's failure as a provider.

Peter Baxter, in an essay that examines the iconic cultural significance of Dietrich's legs, describes the resemblance, both in physique and in dress, between Kiepert and Rath. He concludes that their similarity is fraught with "the kind of tension that ensues when the child's identification with his father leads him to covet his father's prerogatives."[29] While Kiepert is a professor of magic, Rath was a real professor, and Rath's clownish costume apes Kiepert's formal garb, while his treatment of Rath's battered hat signifies castration. The hat is crushed, run through with a dagger and fired at with a pistol, finally releasing a bird. Kiepert's statement, made as the bird flies from the hat, that Rath now has "a weight off his mind," describes Rath's moment of loss.

Rath's deterioration and humiliation, chronicled in costume signs, emphasizes the impossibility of a relationship with Lola (he is not a "real" man; therefore, he cannot be loved by a "real" woman), whose own costumes throughout the film continue to convey inaccessibility. At one point, when she assumes the famous pose in which she leans back grasping her knee, she is wearing a typical cabaret outfit with top hat and black stockings and garters. Her "skirt" is not really a skirt, but a design which appears to have been hiked up and held in place. This affected, conscious exposure constitutes another come-on, and, like previous signposts, points to erotically charged else-wheres. It is a costume made up of many layers (overskirt, frilly underskirt, underpants), several of which have been raised. But Lola's pose (not toward the camera, but sideways), and her song of warning convey her inaccessibility. While she can't help falling in love again, and she is not to blame for those men who burn their wings around her flame, she remains enticing but inaccessible, and that last layer, signified by the unremoved undergarment, will never be peeled away.

Lola's inaccessibility is further punctuated by the film's exclamatory last scene. After Rath returns to his old school in the now-disheveled garb of his professional days, dying at the desk in his empty classroom, Lola appears again on stage in a cabaret costume. This time, however, her posture as well as her costume are more defiant, and she seems more certain of her own ability to maintain distance as she coldly sings an encore of "Falling in Love Again," here facing the audience and straddling a chair placed backwards. As mentioned earlier, the scene expresses Lola's psychological development in its self-realizing message of inaccessibility and distance.[30]

It is clear from Sternberg's first association with Dietrich in *The Blue Angel* that he was beginning to develop, through costume signs and creation of the star, a strategy for exploring the nature of cinema. *Blonde Venus* continues the development of that artistic strategy by elaborating on themes of role-playing and performance introduced in *The Blue Angel*.

Like *The Blue Angel, Blonde Venus* utilizes clothing as an element of mise-en-scène that acts as a metaphorical impediment to cinematic transparency. Here, more than in the earlier *Shanghai Express* and *Morocco,* the exotic locales are an important element in the film's basic tensions, serving as an antithesis to home, and constructing a world in which woman remains both literally and figuratively dislocated. (In *Shanghai Express,* the exotic locale serves as an unfit place for the "notorious white flower," who, because of her racial difference and fetishized physical hyperbole, of whiteness/blondness, does not mesh with her geographical or cultural surroundings. Similar dislocation is reflected in her shifting identities throughout the film.)

Lola-Lola prior to her final rendition of "Falling in Love Again" in *The Blue Angel*. (Photofest)

Lola-Lola in her earlier rendition of "Falling in Love Again." (Photofest)

In *Blonde Venus*, Sternberg broadens the notion of dislocation by defining woman's shifting roles through costume incongruity and gesture, and by structuring the film as a search. While both films explore role-playing as a strategy for layering and distancing, *The Blue Angel* presents the Dietrich character as a woman who knows what she wants, while *Blonde Venus* presents her as a woman in search of self.

Throughout the film, Helen Faraday (Dietrich) is engaged in a search—a search controlled primarily by men (Sternberg, her husband, her agents and managers, her lover, the detective), but sometimes initiated by Helen herself (Helen as performer in control of her own career as distinguished from Helen as performer controlled by men). It is a search that takes her through a variety of woman's roles in an evolutionary process of self-discovery and cultural definition. These roles range from the primitive and pure (Helen as wood nymph), through the biological (Helen as mother), the sociological/cultural (Helen as wife), the professional (Helen as performer), to the sexual (Helen as lover; Helen as prostitute). The final conflicting images signify confusion and tension, and reveal Sternberg's undercutting of, and discomfort with, the notion of the Happy Hollywood Family.

Blonde Venus begins its search with a prologue that situates woman in a mythic, primitive locale and presents her in her natural state of undress, or nudity. Ned Faraday (Herbert Marshall), a student on an outing with some friends in the woods of Bavaria, encounters six "wood nymphs" swimming nude, like mythological mermaids in a pool. The scene is partially obscured by Sternberg's characteristic frame clutter (here in the form of trees, leaves, and branches) and objects shot with gauzy, soft-focus photography. The nymphs are voyeuristically observed by the young men, who share the audience's point of view, and Ned falls immediately in love with the most beautiful one (Dietrich). While her character name is not revealed until the next sequence, the name Helen seems appropriate because of the mythological and historical association of Helen of Troy with irresistible beauty.

Sternberg's introduction of Helen in the nude presents notions of the erotic, the mythological (woman as goddess/siren, which will be later enlarged by Helen as performer/singer), the pure and elemental, the natural and primal states which serve as the starting points for woman's evolutionary search that will continue throughout the film. The sequence, often excluded from contemporary prints because of its excision by the Hays Office in 1934, also serves as a narrative and thematic overture both for the concerns of this particular film and for other Sternbergian interests: the control of pleasure, the tension between revelation and concealment, and woman as object of the male gaze.

The nudity in which Helen the character and Dietrich the star are introduced immediately suggests Sternbergian tensions centered around display and concealment which have been dealt with in earlier films such as *Shanghai Express* and *The Blue Angel.* Here, however, the analogue to the control of display is not, as it was in *The Blue Angel,* the semirevealing costume of the performer, nor, as will be seen in *Shanghai Express,* disguise, but rather, modesty. Her degree of exposure is apparently under Helen's control (she tries to cover up), though by virtue of shot composition (visual clutter and soft focus), it is more accurately under the control of Sternberg. Since modesty is "an inhibitory impulse directed against either social or sexual forms of display,"[31] it serves as a directorial means of controlling the display functions of both star and her cinematic vehicle. For Sternberg, modesty serves a dual inhibitory purpose: it is in opposition not only to the wearing of too few clothes, but also to the wearing of outrageous and spectacular clothes. According to Anne Hollander, the more important clothing is, the more meaningful is its absence.[32]

Thus, the outrageous costumes worn by Dietrich in his films may be viewed as a condition of display which Sternberg attempts to inhibit by keeping Dietrich moving through a variety of roles that do not fit or suit her, or, in the case of *The Blue Angel* and later films (*Dishonored* and *Shanghai Express*) by presenting costume as a means of concealment. The modesty expressed by Helen and Sternberg in this first sequence presents, in capsule form, a characteristic Sternbergian tension: while her nakedness exploits the display function of cinema, his directorial "modesty" serves the same purpose as semirevealing costumes did in *The Blue Angel* by encouraging viewer desire while preventing satisfaction.

Nudity serves a variety of functions both within its cultural/historical/artistic context and within its filmic context. The unadorned body has been idealized as expression of "the longings for a primal virtue, a primal human beauty and sexuality."[33] The discovery of Helen in her primal state suggests a state of pure sexuality and its ensuing desire, both of which are suppressed by the numerous roles that Helen plays throughout the rest of the film. The abrupt transition from Bavarian stream water to New York City bath water, as Helen bathes her son in the film's second scene, suggests the swift transformation of woman when removed from her mythic, primitive locale, and replaced in cultural contexts which constantly trap her in a variety of unsatisfying roles. In this first shot after the prologue, Helen appears disheveled, and Dietrich-as-mother delivers several unconvincing maternal lines. Sternberg, in fact, was virulently opposed to the characterization of Dietrich-as-mother, and his objection caused him to resign as director early in the production.[34] He only rescinded this resignation when Dietrich refused to work with anyone else, declaring, "Von for all and all for Von!" In the role of mother, Dietrich is contextually and culturally out of place here, and her dislocation is reflected in demeanor (costume, hairstyle, posture), dialogue and performance.

Nudity as purity serves a second idealizing function in its relationship to the myth of Adam and Eve, which illustrates the concept of naturally virtuous nudity.[35] Such a notion works in relation to the mythic, idyllic, Edenic setting of the first encounter between Ned and Helen, but one must remember the drastic alteration of man's originally perfect state and the need to conceal nudity after his fall.[36] Additionally, behind the figures of Adam and Eve stand the figures of Venus and Adonis, exemplifying human sexuality.[37] The film's title, which refers to Helen's stage name, implies this sexuality and her loss of innocence in her role as a performer later in the film.

As the opposite of nudity and woman's natural state, the dressing of Helen can be seen as a metaphor for the process of acculturation, the "dressing" of woman in various roles, many of which are unsuitable. Some anthropologists believe that it was male jealousy that endowed women with clothes: "In some primitive communities, it was the married woman who was clothed in order to conceal her body from other men's eyes."[38] Clearly, Sternberg and Ned suffer from the same impulse. While Sternberg uses costume to control viewer pleasure, Ned uses rigid role definitions to control Helen's natural sexuality, attempting to maintain her position in the family as de-sexualized mother/wife. It is a position from which he later displaces Helen when he attacks her motherhood and takes her son, Johnny, from her.

Both Helen's and Sternberg's exhibitionistic impulse to draw attention to the body and to display its charms is a natural tendency found in all people.[39] As an element of cinematic spectacle, it later takes the form of professional exhibitionism: Helen is a performer, always on display; it is a profession which she gives up for motherhood and family, but one to which she constantly returns for financial sustenance. Since a primary purpose of costume is to serve this display function,[40] it seems reasonable for Sternberg to have adopted costume as a means of both enhancing and controlling the tendency.

Another example of nudity occurs in the film's second scene as

Helen-as-mother with Ned (Herbert Marshall) in *Blonde Venus*. (Photofest)

the child is bathed by his mother. The parallels to the first sequence are unmistakable: nudity, playfulness, enjoyment, water, a dissolve from Bavarian stream water to New York City bath water. All serve to restate the innocence and purity of the first scene while also qualifying it. While purity and innocence are apparently transferred to the home, one wonders what is missing from this picture. It is, of course, Helen as sex object. Sternberg is presenting a seemingly normal family existence, but with numerous signals that undercut support for the traditional Hollywood family. The similarities to and differences from the opening sequence foreground the suppression of eroticism within the home, while the film's "distaste for the nuclear family"[41] emerges, as Robin Wood suggests, in the behavior of the child: he plays with toys that have sexual connotations (guns, rifles, trumpets) and later has these toys taken away from him; he is placed in a crib, though old enough to sleep in a bed.[42] The suppression of the erotic, which continues throughout the film as a conflict among woman's roles (performer/sexual object vs. mother/wife/repressed sexuality) is here emphasized by the retelling of the story of their first meeting as a bedtime fairy tale for the couple's son, Johnny. It is a sexual fantasy (it is about erotic contemplation, voyeurism, and pleasure, and has obviously been repeated often to satisfy the child's desire) sanitized by the physical relocation of characters (now in the nursery) and the cultural redefinition of their roles (sexual object to mother; student-voyeur to father).

As the parents relate the story of their meeting—a carefully desexualized tale of Ned's seduction of Helen-the-singing-Siren—they respond to Johnny's demands for more information (his repeated question, "And *then* what happened?" reflects a kind of verbal voyeurism) by concealing the sexual nature of their relationship. They behave like "good parents" and protect Johnny from the erotic truth. While Ned seems about to continue the story's details in more specific, more honest terms ("And then we kissed. . . . And then . . ."), Helen, her hand covering Ned's mouth, prevents him from completing it. As a result of his muzzling, Ned jumps to the culturally acceptable purpose of sexual encounter, i.e., procreation, in his completion of the story, ("And then we started to think about you, Johnny"). The repetition of this sexual fantasy/fairy tale at the film's conclusion and Sternberg's use of the story as a sign of the couple's reconciliation, further emphasizes the necessity for the suppression of the erotic and sexual in the maintenance of the family while also creating a picture of dislocation.

The antiglamorous presentation of Dietrich in housedress, as well as the abrupt transition from wood nymph to hausfrau, from performer

to mother, is disappointing when one considers what was promised by
the first scene. The titillating nudity, sexuality, eroticism, voyeurism
and fetishism are teasingly reproduced in small doses with the introduction of the child, and then removed, altered, suppressed or de-
glamorized. The naked child exists at the opposite end of the modesty/
immodesty scale from the adult. In the child, there is no attempt to
conceal genitalia or maintain privacy or modesty. Thus, the shift from
woman to child, indicated by the dissolve, suggests regression to a state
of innocence that "parallels that state of existence in the Garden of
Eden before man became aware of his individuality."[43] This awareness
of individuality, an acknowledgment of one's sexual difference, recognized by Ned in their first meeting, suppressed by the family and reflected throughout in costume signs, will be later rediscovered by
Helen and exploited by her to achieve personal, financial and sexual
independence from the societal roles that limit her.

Helen's discomfort with mothering in a repressive family structure
continues to grow with Ned's refusal to allow her to work, i.e.,
return to the stage, in order to help him obtain money for an operation he needs to save his life. She wants to alter her role from mother/
wife to performer/provider and it is this desire that motivates her
ensuing search. While apparently self-motivated, it must be remembered that Helen is committed to saving her husband and preserving
the family. Helen is able to succeed in making a business deal at
which her husband has failed. She is able to sell her body, which is
eagerly purchased by men who employ and observe her, while his
body, offered to science in exchange for much-needed money for his
family, is rejected by a doctor who doesn't want it. Sternberg's irony
here is a measure of his own amusement.

The next step in her search takes Helen out of the home and role of
mother/wife and into the cabaret and role of performer. Against Ned's
wishes (he understands the threat to the family if the mother/wife is
permitted to venture outside the home), Helen returns to the stage to
find a job. In a brief scene which precedes her search for a job, Helen
is seated at a sewing machine, an iconographical foreshadowing of her
evolutionary search and a suggestion of the preparation for that search
through the creation of costume. As previously mentioned, costume
will serve as metaphor for the various roles she will attempt, i.e., try
on, throughout the rest of the film. Helen's first encounter with a theatrical agent provides an ironic counterpoint to the film's first scene. The
agent asks Helen to show him what she's got. Here Helen must work
against the modesty impulse presented earlier, by displaying her wares;
however, she is "protected" by Sternberg, who obscures the audience's
view of her legs by shooting from behind a desk. Concealment here has

a double edge: Sternberg's apparent paternalism vs. the teasing concealment of Dietrich's famous legs protects her only temporarily. Soon, Helen will perform on stage, and the need to display will tap her natural, exhibitionistic impulse, previously under the control of character modesty and directorial concealment.

In the next scene, Helen is escorted to the theater manager's office, where a deal is made by the agent and manager and control of Helen's destiny is placed in the hands of men. While Helen awaits the decision on her contract, she stands next to a nude female statue, uncomfortably adjusting her own fur collar in an attempt to protect herself from the gaze of the men who watch her. The presence of the nude statue highlights Helen's feelings of exposure and reminds us of Sternberg's earlier depiction of nakedness and the impulse to conceal it. In an interesting costume gesture, the agent drops his hat over the head of the statue, emphasizing the value of the rest of woman's body and the relative unimportance of her head/mind/will in the world of display, performance and desire which Helen is about to enter. Additionally, by placing the hat over the statue's head and arms, obscuring both from view, the agent has created a Venus de Milo foreshadowing Helen's role in her upcoming cabaret debut.

The dressing room is a favorite locale for Sternberg's performers. Typically, Sternberg's dressing rooms are cluttered with costumes, props and makeup—the signs of masquerade, disguise and performance which provide his star with the material required for the many roles she will play, both on stage and within the context of her character's personal life. In fact, performance is a metaphor for Helen's endless search to find herself, a search which leads nowhere, since Helen never really finds a self. She finds only a succession of roles, the authenticity of which is systematically undermined by the exposure, not the celebration, of every myth of woman presented by the film and by the male dominance which determines her roles.[44]

In the film's first dressing room scene, Helen prepares for her role as the Blonde Venus. On her table stands a photograph of Johnny, serving as a visual reminder of the conflict between her role as erotic performer (the cabaret's neon sign invites the audience to "come early and stay late") and her role as de-sexualized mother. In this scene, Sternberg uses costume-related dialogue to further emphasize themes of revelation/concealment and truth/illusion. In stating his knowledge of Taxi Belle Hooper's attachment to Nick Townsend, the manager verbalizes themes previously introduced by costume imagery:

Manager: Nick just came in.
Taxi: Why tell me?
Manager: You're not pulling any wool over *my* eyes.

Helen (with Taxi Belle Hooper) prepares for her role as the Blonde Venus. (Photofest)

While dressing is a metaphor for role-playing, undressing is a metaphor for revelation. Undressing in front of an audience places woman on display for erotic contemplation. Sternberg extends the metaphor even further, and perhaps most interestingly, in the "Hot Voodoo" number performed by Helen in her role as the Blonde Venus; it is here that undressing and the removal of costume becomes an act of striptease, an act that parallels the process of cinematic revelation, which, in characteristic Sternbergian style, often promises more than it delivers. In the language of costume, film is a striptease, a peeling away of layers of information, a slow disclosure of meaning[45] during which layers of deception are often, but not always, removed. Sternberg's use of Dietrich as double agent—as an agent of display (the female star to be contemplated) and as an agent of disguise (she is not always what she appears to be)—embodies an opposition that impedes discovery and maintains a tension between what film promises and what it delivers.

"Hot Voodoo" also seeks to control pleasure by exploiting those tensions between display and concealment. Helen's performance is centered around this tension. As Bill Nichols has suggested, performance

> promises pleasure in a context of presence and absence, hide and seek, offer and withdrawal which establishes a parallel between Sternberg's performance and his character's, between his spectacle and Helen's.[46]

Nichols notes the number's provocative call to pleasure amidst a setting of tropical eroticism and suggests that "the entire film pivots around Helen's struggle to gain control of her performance," since the details and style of Helen's actual performance are not under her control.[47] (This is true until her last performance of the film, when she wears white-tie and tails).

Roland Barthes's discussion of striptease takes the idea of display/concealment tension a step further. For Barthes, striptease involves a contradiction: "Woman is desexualized at the very moment when she is stripped naked"; therefore, the spectacle is based on a fear of sex conjured up by ritual signs of striptease which ultimately "negate the flesh."[48] Barthes's point is that the striptease involves a series of uncoverings, but the woman merely pretends to strip bare. Exoticism and its trappings (i.e., foreignness, furs, fans, gloves, etc.) "aim at establishing the woman as an object in disguise." The end of the striptease, then, is to signify, through the shedding of "incongruous and artificial clothing," nudity or nakedness as woman's perfectly chaste natural state.[49]

The "Hot Voodoo" number supports Barthes's theory in several ways. Both pretense and reassurance are maintained by presenting the ritual of performance within a cabaret. It is a place for erotic display, but within a restrictive filmic context. Audience experience tells the viewer that the promised striptease cannot be completely delivered. Based on movie precedent, it must stop at an acceptably modest moment. Once again, Sternberg exercises control of pleasure by relying on the known restrictions of his medium and on his audience's expectations.

Barthes's theory applies as well to woman's de-sexualized, non-erotic condition in Sternberg's films, a condition described by feminist theorists as one necessary to maintain woman's repression as social/sexual being. It allows man to remain at the center of the film's world, despite its apparent focus on a woman.[50] If woman is immediately established as an object in disguise, both by Sternberg's attempts to clothe her in various identities and roles and by the use of the exotic to serve as barrier to revelation of the "real" woman, then the end of Sternberg's cinematic striptease, like the end of Barthes's striptease, is to present the woman to whom there can be no access—a woman over whom he and the societal restrictions placed on her maintain total control.

With typically Sternbergian perversity, the ape suit that conceals Helen is removed to "reveal" a rather unrevealing costume. While it is brief (much like a contemporary one-piece bathing suit), it is covered with sparkling glitter and fur that distract attention from the body beneath it. Furthermore, Sternberg's camera dollies in closely so as to prevent audience view and appreciation of Dietrich's famed legs. The first fetishistic close-up is of the pseudo-African dancers' legs, and the shot of their suggestively undulating movements is more than we will ever see of Dietrich. In fact, throughout her song, she moves only slightly from side to side; most of the erotic undulation continues only in the background, among the members of the chorus.

Robin Wood has commented on Sternberg's exploitation of the concealment/revelation paradox of the striptease. In discussing "Hot Voodoo," Wood locates tension in the contrast between the scene's background and foreground details:

> "Hot Voodoo" offers the apparent release of the forces that normality represses: beating drums, savagery (African dancers); animalism (gorilla); aggression (exaggerated jagged teeth on native shields); eroticism (Dietrich's glittering, emphasized breasts; the words of the song).[51]

Against all these are counterpoint details:

Helen as the Blonde Venus, having emerged from the ape suit. (Movie Star News)

"Savages" are women on display (chained); the gorilla drags a chain—
nothing is what it seems: the blacks are painted whites; the gorilla is
Dietrich . . . and there is a characteristic Sternbergian sense of constric-
tion, the decor pressing in, dancers and customers crowded together.[52]

There is, however, another interpretation of "Hot Voodoo." If, in
fact, Helen has exercised some degree of control over her decision
to return to the stage, then her striptease can also be read as a public
attempt to shed that which traps her. The metaphorical coverings
(costume, disguise) that seek to classify her in each man's image of
woman (Ned sees her as wife; Nick sees her as concubine; Johnny
sees her as mother) are presented in a parody of evolution, which
Helen seeks to counteract. Her shedding of skins in an apparent strip
suggests an attempt to return to the original, natural state glimpsed
in the film's prologue—a state uninhibited in its nudity by the "civi-
lizing" forces of patriarchally imposed roles and their metaphorical
clothing restrictions. It is Sternberg and the restrictions of the com-

mercial film medium that prevent Helen from reclaiming her state of primal innocence and freedom, but, as Robin Wood has noted, it is the men in the film who continually trap her in unwanted roles, as housewife, mother or kept woman.[53]

In a brilliant overture of the film's narrative structure, using the striptease as metaphor for Helen's struggles with role-identification throughout the film, "Hot Voodoo" presents the evolutionary search for self-discovery through its rich costume signs.

The creature that ultimately emerges from the ape suit, i.e., the Blonde Venus, serves as a variation on the idea of the dislocated woman presented in *Shanghai Express*. She is white (against a background chorus of "black" women); blonde (wearing an exaggerated wig); and glamorous (her glitter and fur against a primitive, pagan background). Her difference is highlighted and her allure accentuated for those men who observe her. Like Lola-Lola's performance in *The Blue Angel*, Helen's "feminine atavism,"[54] highly stylized in "Hot Voodoo," connotes the bizarre, the dangerous, the barbaric.

Once again, as in previous films, Sternberg links beauty with danger. Both in terms of costume and narrative context, Helen is transformed into what Bill Nichols has dubbed a "Venus Fur Trap." Nichols is referring here to a particular portion of Helen's costume— "the heart-shaped, fur covering that extends from waist to groin"— which is designed to create a seductive game of "hide-and-seek" and a "symptomatic manifestation of the psychodynamics of erotic contemplation."[55] Here, as in *The Blue Angel*, Sternberg identifies the fatal woman through her costumes, while presenting her in a format that places those who contemplate and desire her in a dangerous position—a position with potential for rejection, destruction, and humiliation. While Helen is, throughout *Blonde Venus*, not the active femme fatale of *The Blue Angel*, *Dishonored* or *Shanghai Express*, she does later evolve into a parody of a man-hating androgyne in white-tie and tails who "takes 'em like Grant took Richmond."

In the dressing room scene that follows "Hot Voodoo," Helen is visited by three admirers. As she prepares for her next number, Nick Townsend (Cary Grant) expresses an interest in her. She dons a toy soldier's hat as Nick offers to be of financial help to her; he has noticed Johnny's photograph and the doll on which the Blonde Venus wig has been placed (a sign of Helen's maternal/professional conflict). Sternberg again utilizes the soldier's uniform to express an independence of spirit, though this independence cannot be maintained by Helen. She has no choice but to accept the check offered to her by Townsend so that she can help her family. After the "purchase" by Townsend, Helen begins to wear more expensive clothes, and especially after her husband leaves for Europe, her clothes are nearly always trimmed with fur collars or cuffs. Here, the use of fur is more a sign of luxury than the symbol of power it was in *Shanghai Express*. Helen's clothes are more expensive and glamorous while she is with Townsend, and are discernibly different from the drab frocks associated with her roles as wife and mother. However, although she is clearly under the financial control of Townsend, she has chosen this position as an act of personal sacrifice for her family. Helen sells her body with the awareness of its marketability. It is clear that she is worth more as an illegitimately kept woman than she is as a legitimately kept wife, and her fur-trimmed costume reflects this difference.

Paradoxically, Helen's greatest source of power is also her Achilles heel. Woman's biological potential to bear children and the magical power invested in them for this ability implies a threat to patriarchy, so when patriarchy strikes back, it attempts to remove her maternal power. When Ned returns to discover that Helen has been having an affair, he tries to take Johnny away from her. Helen's ensuing flight with Johnny takes her through a series of ordeals marked by degradation and desperation. During these ordeals her costume changes dramatically from glamorous to tasteless, from lavish to sor-

Helen in patchwork shawl, part of her streetwalker attire. (Jerry Ohlinger)

Helen in her toy soldier's hat, with Nick (Cary Grant). (Jerry Ohlinger)

Helen in one of the more lavish dresses purchased for her by Nick. (Jerry Ohlinger)

did, paralleling the changes in her life-style. Though she continues to wear fur, it has become increasingly shabby. (Her tattered scarves, however, only suggest the rags that Banton clearly could not have dressed his star in.) At one point, she wears a patchwork shawl, a stylized sign of destitution that substitutes for a more complete and accurate picture of indigence.

During her flight with Johnny, Helen meets another mother whose warning helps her. This woman's costume and demeanor suggest the shared difficulties of women bound by roles and ideological stereotypes. The woman is the proprietor of a nightclub in which Helen works, and she dresses in stereotypical Lesbian attire (a masculine suit and tie; short, close-cut hair; "tough" demeanor). She warns Helen about her pursuers, expressing sympathy as a mother and promising silence as to Helen's whereabouts ("Don't worry—I've got a kid, too"). The suggestion here is that in becoming successful in a man's world (all previous nightclub owners have been men), a woman must become as much like a man as possible. It is a foreshadowing of Helen's later success as a performer, when she appears in white-tie and tails, taking control of both her own life and of the emotions of those who suffer rejection by her.

In another of Sternberg's dressing rooms, Johnny wears a full-faced mask on the back of his head. Again, the child is presented ambiguously. Often a symbol of deception, the mask here can be read as a sign of Johnny's duality: he is, ultimately, the force that maintains the fairy tale's life, while his needs and very existence strangle Helen's. Like the two-faced Roman deity, Janus, who presides over beginnings, Johnny is the motivating force behind the maintenance of the nuclear family (the fairy tale) and his power is most visible in his effect on both parents' actions (the struggle for custody, the flight to prevent his loss, their final reconciliation), and on their continuing relationship. Johnny is Sternberg's little manipulator—and one he doesn't trust, based on the mask and other aforementioned signs of brutality and his darker side. It is clearly the child who keeps the fairy tale nuclear family going when, in the film's last scene, he maintains the movement of the carousel toy, symbolic of his parents' romantic meeting and ensuing relationship, by pushing it along with his hand. The maintenance of the fairy tale by this ambiguous child again highlights Sternberg's discomfort with the happy nuclear family, a discomfort supported by Dietrich's magnificent final costume and Sternberg's shooting of the film's final scene.

The impossibility of real reconciliation is an idea that defies traditional Hollywood happy endings as well as the apparent ending of

Blonde Venus. However, such an impossibility may be suggested by the contradiction between Helen's glamorous, erotic gown (décolleté neckline, plunging back) and the way Sternberg shoots the scene (Helen is the object of the camera's gaze, as well as of Ned's; Helen's plunging neckline is carefully obscured by a portion of Johnny's crib).

Helen in her last costume, just before she sees Johnny. (Jerry Ohlinger)

As E. Ann Kaplan has suggested, "Dietrich's clothes betray the fundamental contradiction between fetishism and mothering that underlies the whole film."[56] Sternberg himself questions Helen's fitness as a mother, but from a position which differs from society's brutal challenge of her maternity within the film's narrative. It is not, for Sternberg, Helen's life-style that interferes with biological/maternal fitness, but rather the repressiveness of the family and its consequential de-sexualization of a naturally sexual being (cf. the film's prologue). As Helen and Ned retell the fairy tale—the analogue to the encounter-romance-marriage-child cycle visually represented by the toy carousel—contradictory images emphasize the difficulty of its continuation. Ned claims that he has forgotten the story, and Johnny, in an admonishing tone, continues it himself by feeding lines to his parents. As Helen sings her lullaby again, Sternberg's cutting from Helen to Ned to Johnny suggests that Ned's acquiescence may be a mixture of sexual longing and parental responsibility.

Undoubtedly the costume that has received the most critical attention in *Blonde Venus* is the white-tie and tails worn by Helen in her triumphant appearance as the Toast of Paris. Her rejection of the last remnant of marital dependency, i.e., Ned's repayment of money she earned to help him arrange his necessary medical treatment, is followed by a series of dissolves that announce her own success. Helen has made it, and she has done so on her own.

Helen as the Toast of Paris in white tie and tails. (Jerry Ohlinger)

Sternberg puts Dietrich in a costume that closely resembles the tuxedo she wore in *Morocco*, and he hints again at Lesbianism by having Helen pinch the cheeks of her chorus girls and by dialogue references which describe her as "cold as the proverbial iceberg." But this costume has its own integrity, since it allegorically represents another stage in Helen's search. Engaged in a search for her sexual and social identity, constantly trying on various roles for their suitability, Helen ultimately becomes the androgyne, a sexually indefinite being. The vagueness of the role seems comfortable for Helen after so many prior rigid role definitions. Carolyn Heilbrun suggests the liberating aspects of androgyny:

> Androgyny suggests . . . a full range of experience open to individuals . . . it suggests a spectrum upon which human beings choose their places without regard to propriety or custom.[57]

For Helen, who has suffered through a series of ill-suited roles, androgyny represents the discovery of a self without social restriction or sexual limitations. In defining the nature of androgyny, Heilbrun quotes from Thomas Rosenmeyer's description of the androgynous Dionysus in Euripides' *The Bacchae:*

> Dionysus appears to be neither woman nor man; or better, he presents himself as woman-in-man or man-in-woman, the unlimited personality. . . . In the person of the god strength mingles with softness, majestic terror with coquettish glances.[58]

While discarding the ape suit suggested a change from male to female, the evolution to androgyny represents, for Helen, a movement toward free choice and away from sexual and social stereotyping, a limitless personality who combines the dualistic characteristics of the androgynous Dionysus in her performance.

Androgyny, both historically and as represented in art, has been signified by cross-dressing, and women have often turned to cross-dressing as a means of attempted liberation from the restrictions of patriarchal structures. Susan Gubar comments on the androgynous clothing chosen by women she interviewed in an Indian prison:

> . . . their costumes were a survival strategy, even a form of escape: unable to alter their imprisonment, these women transformed themselves.[59]

Gubar uses the example to better clarify our understanding of the role clothing plays in the response of women to confinement within patriarchal restrictions.[60]

Cross-dressing has also served to signify the achievement of status for women who have "made it" in a man's world. Gubar refers to the clothing worn by Dr. Mary Walker, a writer and spokesperson for women's rights at the turn of the century:

[Dr.] Walker ostentatiously dressed up in male costumes not just for comfort and dignity, but to appropriate and display conventionally male attainments and status.[61]

Both of the above references support the choice of cross-dressing in *Blonde Venus*, for while Helen has achieved professional status, she has also rejected the confining accoutrements of mother, wife and sexual object.

Still enticing and mysterious, Helen has become unapproachable and inaccessible in her coldness, i.e., frigidity. The discovery of her sense of self has also required a corresponding self-imposed isolation, a setting-apart of the self from the society that has previously trapped her. The message written on her dressing room mirror says: "Down to Gehenna or up to the throne, he travels fastest who travels alone," and Helen's choice has left her the solitary traveler. As Rebecca Bell-Metereau has pointed out in her study of Hollywood androgyny:

> The androgyne has long been the mythic symbol of wisdom and self-sufficiency—a figure whose in-between status inspires fascination, dread, reverence. In our own culture, priests and nuns have historically striven for angelic wisdom by denying their sexuality and forfeiting participation in the gender-related rituals of mating and procreating.[62]

Like the androgyne described above, Helen has, in her establishment of self-sufficiency, exercised a denial of her own sexuality and a forfeit of her maternal, procreational roles, a sacrifice she ultimately cannot live with. Her ambivalence surfaces in the dressing room scene that follows her performance. Here she is reminded by Nick of her motherhood ("You care more about Johnny than anything else on earth"). While she initially rejects his offer to return to New York, popping her top hat in a gesture of casual indifference that masks true feelings, the next shot of a newspaper story announcing her engagement to Nick and their return to New York conveys her dramatic change of heart and her assent to maternity.

Helen's white-tie and tails can be viewed as well as Sternberg's return to his fascination with disguise, a recapitulation of the costume metaphor that structures the narratives of *Dishonored* and *Shanghai Express*, as well as the later comedies, *The King Steps Out* and *Jet Pilot*. It might be interesting, however, to note the differences between *Blonde Venus* and *Shanghai Express*. While the narrative structure of *Shanghai Express* centers around disguise, the Paris cabaret scene in *Blonde Venus* is more accurately about masquerade. Disguise, the attempt to conceal the identity or integrity of the self, is a form of camouflage designed to obscure what *is:* its object is deception. Thus Helen has, in her flight as a fugitive, used disguise as a means to elude her pursuers. Masquerade, on the other hand, implies impersonation, an attempt to live or act under false pretenses. Its object is often entertainment rather than deception. Helen is fooling no one in her white-tie and tails—surely no member of either Sternberg's cabaret audience nor anyone in the audience who views the film is deceived by Helen's masquerade. The masquerade is merely at attempt to highlight what is *not*, to foreground the other (Helen's sexual ambiguity suggests her "otherness"). It constructs a tension between display, the presentation of the fetishized object, and Sternberg's control of viewer desire (which he encourages) and viewer pleasure (which he impedes through his use of costume).

Sexual masquerade is a way of misrepresenting sexual difference and another measure of Sternberg's directorial play. While Helen/Dietrich has, both as character and star, been the object of contemplation throughout the film, her appearance as androgyne is an attempt to subvert that identification. E. Ann Kaplan suggests that Helen's "masculinization allows subversive female-female bonding, as Dietrich fondles a chorus girl, using masquerade to 'legitimize' the attraction."[63] Here, she combines being on display with a subversive female-female bonding that is very different from objectification. Such female bonding, Kaplan suggests, "excludes men and subverts patriarchal domination."[64]

Kaplan comments further on how Helen/Dietrich is fetishized in her final Paris performance. She becomes an isolated image in the frame that offers "erotic connection for the male spectator."[65]

Both Kaplan's idea and the notion of masquerade support the *Cahiers* critics' assertion of woman as pseudocenter of the filmic discourse. Elaborating on this theory, Claire Johnston suggests that in order to maintain the male at the center of the universe in a film which focuses on woman, the director must repress the idea of woman as social/sexual being, denying the man/woman opposition completely:

The real opposition posed by the sign is male/non-male, which Sternberg establishes by his use of masculine clothing enveloping the image of Dietrich. This masquerade indicates the absence of man, an absence that is simultaneously negated and recuperated by man. The image of the woman becomes merely the trace of the exclusion and repression of Woman.[66]

What Johnston and other feminist theorists have not considered in regard to *Blonde Venus* is the fact that the film does not unquestioningly construct woman as object of the male gaze. It is Helen herself who, though her options are ultimately confined by patriarchy, initiates almost every major narrative development.[67] In fact, the film highlights the impossibility of "discovery" in woman's evolutionary search, an idea that supports feminist theory.

As Robin Wood has stated in his discussion of *Blonde Venus*:

> . . . true femininity cannot yet exist, since all available roles for women in society are determined by male dominance. Every myth of woman is exposed in the film, not celebrated. It also constitutes an astonishingly comprehensive analysis of the manifold forms of prostitution—from the home to the doss house—available to woman in our culture.[68]

Blonde Venus stands as Sternberg's most complete acknowledgment regarding woman's condition in society and the hopelessness of her search for a sense of self. Through the use of costume to chart her evolution, he has created a picture feminist in its observation, radical in its despair.

4

Deception, Spying and Disguise: *Dishonored, Shanghai Express, The King Steps Out* and *Jet Pilot*

Dishonored (1931) was the first of four Sternberg/Dietrich films to use costume, specifically disguise, as a central metaphor for deception. In *Shanghai Express*, the film which followed *Dishonored*, the disguise created mystery and ambiguity, maintaining inaccessibility despite the seeming accessibility of the film image. Later, Sternberg would return to disguise and deception, viewing the subjects comedically in the non-Dietrich films *The King Steps Out* (1936) and *Jet Pilot* (1951).

Dishonored's central theme explores deception in its various aspects: professional, political and sexual. Sternberg is also interested in the reevaluation of deception as honor, an idea he investigates through the Dietrich character and her "honorable" role as a spy. The title, while not approved by Sternberg (it was changed from his original story title, "X-27," by studio executives), is ultimately ironic. As Sternberg protested, "the lady spy was not dishonored, but killed by a firing squad."[1] In fact, the traditional military concept of honor is directly challenged by Sternberg, who views Dietrich's sacrifice for love as even more honorable than the sacrifice for one's country.

The story concerns an officer's widow (Dietrich) who has become a prostitute and is offered a chance to redeem herself through an act of patriotism. She becomes X-27, the superspy, whose task is to use her charm and beauty as a prostitute to discover military secrets for the state. One traitor (Warner Oland) who falls prey to her charms kills himself rather than face exposure and public humiliation. Later she meets a fellow spy and enemy officer (Victor McLaglen) with whom she falls in love. Following a series of captures and escapes, McLaglen is finally identified, and, in a moment that expresses the triumph of the erotic over the patriotic, Dietrich allows him to escape. This ensures her own fate as a traitor, but permits Sternberg to express his definition of honor in sexual, rather than political, terms. For X-27 dies for her man, not for her country, the values of which Sternberg seriously questions in the film's final scene.

The film's opening images convey Sternberg's interest in the erotic. A view of Dietrich's legs from the thighs down sectionalizes her body as she adjusts her wrinkled black stockings, attaching them to her garter. The shot is reminiscent of several in *The Blue Angel* and serves a number of purposes. As in the earlier film, the image of Dietrich's legs carries an erotic charge that stimulates desire through its exposure of undergarments and gestures usually performed in private. In their association with undefended nudity higher up, or as signals to the lingerie above, Dietrich's fetishized legs and her gestures of adjustment intensify the voyeuristic interest of the viewer through their promise of more. In addition, the shot refers directly to the famous Dietrich legs, an erotic sign which, in terms of publicity, was reaching iconic proportions. The image promises to continue the erotic journey where *The Blue Angel* left off, but Sternberg will not deliver on that promise. Because of their association with the earlier film, the black stockings and garters become Dietrich's "special stage suit," an outfit instantly recognizable as the star's. As Anne Hollander has noted, such a suit idealizes its wearer, making him or her an object of worship.[2]

The repetition of the special stage suit in this film, after its initial introduction in *The Blue Angel*, identifies it more closely with Dietrich than with a particular character and permits instant audience identification of the star before any associations can be formed with an individual character. In addition, it emphasizes Dietrich's permanence as a persona, even in the presence of the most elaborate role-playing of her career.

Her adjustment completed, Dietrich turns, displaying her fur-trimmed hemline, and Sternberg cuts to a medium shot of his star, whose back is to the camera and whose face, as she turns seductively to look at the camera, is still partially concealed by a huge fur collar, cloche hat, and veil. It is a shadowy, semirevealing introduction, one that Sternberg used earlier in *Morocco* and would repeat again in *Shanghai Express*. In all three instances, he uses gesture, costume, camera set-up and lighting to create a visual impediment to the accessibility promised by star billing. In addition, her profession (she is clearly a streetwalker) presents her as accessible, while his enigmatic star and her complex characterization belie such an impression.

The richness of the opening images also provides references to the film's major theme, i.e., deception, through its play with Dietrich's

Dietrich as streetwalker, her first and last costume in *Dishonored*. (Museum of Modern Art Film Stills Archive)

physical appearance and her essential inner reality. Deception is elaborated on immediately in the film's next scene. After the police remove the body of a prostitute who has committed suicide, establishing the fate of the streetwalker, Dietrich is approached by a potential customer (Gustav von Seyffertitz); he is actually not a customer at all, but the head of the Secret Service, and tries to enlist her assistance as a spy. In a test of her loyalty, he identifies himself as a traitor to Austria. She expresses interest, but after she leaves, ostensibly to get some wine, she returns with a policeman who arrests von Seyffertitz. This loyalty test, which backfires on the exasperated Secret Service man, develops the theme of deception through mistaken identity, a theme that will be explored throughout the rest of the film in costume signs and through the structural metaphor of deception through spying. Dietrich's willingness to turn in a traitor here will be later contrasted to her unwillingness to turn in the traitor she loves. The contrast shows Sternberg's differentiation between types of honor (sexual vs. political) and his reevaluation of the conflict between personal and political commitment.

Also of interest in this scene is an indirect reference to the significance of the uniform in establishing identity. Von Seyffertitz, out of uniform here, is disguised as a customer. Because of this masquerade, he is unrecognizable to the military policeman who arrests him. The implication is that the uniform defines the man and that not wearing it can result in mistaken identity. Later, Sternberg subverts his association of the uniform with loyalty by presenting a traitor who wears one. Sternberg's apparent schizophrenia is no careless contradiction; instead, it reveals a greater interest in the redefinition of the notion of a uniform. When, at the end of the film, Dietrich herself redefines the meaning of the uniform and its relationship to sacrifice and honor (a point which will be elaborated upon later in this chapter), Sternberg's challenge to its traditional significance highlights his equation of military and political power with sexual power while reevaluating conventional definitions of honor and patriotism.

Actually, the uniform appears frequently in Sternberg's films (see, for example, *The Last Command, Morocco, Shanghai Express, The King Steps Out,* and *Jet Pilot*). Its appearance in *Dishonored* specifically prepares for its later use in *Sergeant Madden* (1939), a Wallace Beery vehicle Sternberg was assigned to direct in order to fulfill a contract with M-G-M. In *Sergeant Madden,* the choice presented to the main character, the policeman played by Beery, is between love for his criminally fugitive son and devotion to duty, a choice made clearer by the uniform that defines Beery's character. In *Sergeant Madden,* unlike *Dishonored,* love is subordinated to duty, and Beery's choice is qualified by the replacement of the recalcitrant natural son with a morally superior adopted son who graduates from the police academy to follow in his father's footsteps.

In *Dishonored*'s next scene, Dietrich appears at military headquarters, having been summoned by the previously deceived head of the Secret Service. His acknowledgment of her skill at deception makes her enlistment as a spy seem appropriate, while it furthers the film's major theme.

> Von Seyffertitz: You completely fooled me—had me arrested. You're a
> clever woman and a very loyal one.
> Dietrich: What appeals to me is the chance to serve my country.
> Von Seyffertitz: It is my duty to point out that the profession of a spy
> is the most ignoble calling on earth—lower than anything you may
> have ever experienced. And it is dangerous, of course.
> Dietrich: I've had an inglorious life. It may become my good fortune to
> have a glorious death.

Dietrich's spy work as X-27 begins, appropriately in terms of costume signs, at a masquerade ball. She wears a spectacular Banton creation: a mask and the costume of a Greek warrior, complete with sequins and a plumed helmet. It is in this scene that the theme of deception through disguise is further developed. Dietrich's Greek costume is appropriate to her work: as the ancient Greeks deceived the unwitting Trojans with the stratagem of the wooden horse, so will X-27 deceive those unwitting men who fall prey to her own form of deception and strategy.

X-27 (Dietrich) as Greek warrior for the masquerade ball (with Warner Oland as Hindau and Victor McLaglen as Lieutenant Kranau). (Museum of Modern Art Film Stills Archive)

Sternberg's frames have never been more cluttered than they are in this scene. Streamers, balloons and partying people fill the space with visual material creating, along with the costumes, a masquerade of mise-en-scène that serves to obscure the image. Other guests wear costumes that are often difficult to identify (except for those of the many clowns and ballerinas). The costumes of primary interest (besides Dietrich's) are those worn by men on whom X-27 is to spy. Victor McLaglen, later revealed as Lieutenant Kranau, a spy from the enemy Russian army, is dressed as a clown, but there is evidence that this clown may not be as fun-loving as one might think. His black mask contains the emblem of a skull and crossbones, and he relies on crutches to help him get around. John Baxter has suggested that Sternberg's combination of clown and cripple "adds a mocking quality to the scene,"[3] setting up the later revelation of Kranau-as-spy, and Kranau as X-27's eventual lover and nemesis. As an extension of the theme of deception, X-27 later learns that she has been fooled by the seemingly innocent passing of a cigarette, a gesture that has concealed the exchange of secret information. Ironically, too, this clown is no fool. Here Sternberg has a chance to oppose appearance to reality, whereas in a later film *(The Scarlet Empress)*, the clown-as-cripple is less ironic than directly commentative.

The metaphor of the masquerade-as-means-of-deception has more specific significance in terms of the Sternbergian schema. The masquerade appears again in *The Devil Is A Woman*, while the use of masks fascinates Sternberg in *Blonde Venus*. Here the mask is explored in ways that highlight its historical significance. In addition to its function as a means of disguise, the mask serves as a symbol of alienation, protecting the wearer from harm.[4]

Interestingly, Lieutenant Kranau's mask is blown off when he sneezes, a sneeze provoked by confetti thrown at him by X-27. His frantic gestures to replace his disguise suggest the importance of maintaining the secrecy of his identity. Kranau is the most secretive of the three main characters at the ball. (Also present and in disguise is General von Hindau, played by Warner Oland.) Other than this one lapse, Kranau retains his mask, while both Hindau and X-27 remove theirs. The reading points to the vulnerability of Hindau vs. the impenetrability of Kranau, while Dietrich's removal of her mask exposes her beauty, allowing her to get on with her work.

Another historical association of the mask further explains Sternberg's fascination with it. The mask as symbol of transformation serves as a metaphor for the duality of the actor, a concept that interested Sternberg both in terms of the creation and presentation of his star, and also in terms of his need to control what he viewed as the actor's impulse to freely reveal those emotions that most people keep hidden.[5]

Actors wore masks in Greek theater, and, in his many references to masks, Sternberg appears to have understood their association with acting as well as their signification of duality. According to Oto Bihalji-Merin, in his study of the mask's historical significance,

Man puts the mask on his face and transforms himself through invocation and identification. [The wearer] is himself yet someone else. Madness has touched him—something of the mystery of the raving God, of a spirit of double existence, which resides in masks, and whose last descendant is the actor.[6]

Sternberg's fascination with the idea of roles and role-playing seems understandable. He needed to control, among other things, his star's accessibility, and keeping Dietrich elusive by making her a moving target in an endless number of roles was a strategy he employed regularly (cf. *Blonde Venus* and *The Blue Angel*). While Dietrich's roles differ from film to film, they are never more diversified within a single film than they are in *Dishonored*.[7]

Multiple role-playing in a single film, with its self-conscious fakery and disguise, subverts credible characterization, emphasizing the star behind the characters. What remains is the myth of Dietrich, far too powerful to be subordinated to diffused characterization with no credibility. Thus, role-playing in *Dishonored* represents another attempt to maintain distance and inaccessibility by emphasizing the myth.

Hindau's black executioner's costume, embossed with a heart, foreshadows the fate of its wearer. When he learns, after falling prey to his own emotions and Dietrich's beauty, that he has been deceived by X-27 and will be exposed as a traitor, he becomes his own executioner, preferring to shoot himself rather than die an ignominious death by firing squad. Wearing his officer's uniform, he ceremoniously surrenders his sword to X-27 ("I don't know to whom I would rather surrender"), acknowledging her military victory as well as her sexual triumph. As Joyce Rheuben has suggested, Dietrich's sexual power is often translated into military or political power,[8] and Alexander Walker notes a similar association of Dietrich with military signs, such as the salutes she receives from soldiers who recognize that she wears the same uniform as they.[9]

And Ethan Mordden stresses, in the Dietrich persona, the importance of honor in the elimination of old virgin/whore dichotomies.

> The old distinction that puts women of sensuality on one side of a heavy line and good women on the other dissolves, for Dietrich embodies so many honorable qualities that the distinction is no longer operable. She is a female version of the Douglas Fairbanks hero: chivalrous, bold and sexy.[10]

Dietrich's association with a military code[11] is evident throughout Sternberg's work. In *Morocco*, she associates herself with a foreign legion of women who are given no medals for their bravery, and wear no uniforms to show their affiliation; in *Shanghai Express*, her code of honor is acknowledged by the rebel general, who recognizes her as a soldier. But *Dishonored* pays homage to it most directly. For it is here that traditional notions of honor are directly challenged by the woman who chooses to die for love, her own brand of honor; her code is starkly contrasted to the empty causes that strip men of their humanity and prevent them from acknowledging their own passions.

In the scene following Hindau's suicide, X-27 enters a gambling casino dressed in a glamorous stain lamé gown, black coat and lush fur collar. She is greeted by the other streetwalkers as "Mary," the only time in the film that we actually hear her referred to by a name other than "X-27." It is here that she again encounters Kranau, now disguised in the uniform of an Austrian aviator. At her urging, he bets on number 27 at roulette and loses. Thus far, the uniforms in this film (other than those worn by incidental characters) have been worn by either traitors (Hindau) or spies (Kranau), and the association of the uniform with deception furthers Sternberg's distrust of its usual significance and prepares for his redefinition of its meaning.

Kranau is both aware of and excited by the scent of danger he associates with X-27. He thinks of death "as a beautiful young woman wearing flowers," and buys her roses to literalize his fantasy. When he discovers her identity as X-27, he reveals his own masquerade—a safe disclosure, since he has already disconnected her telephone and removed the bullets from her pistol. Their dialogue exchange is noteworthy here, since it relates specifically to disguise and masquerade, and introduces the double standard that Sternberg will later question.

> Kranau: Do you like this masquerade as well as my last one?
> X-27: You're still a clown.
> Kranau: I'm a colonel in the Russian Army, and when necessary, I fly across the line and play the clown or the Austrian officer. I'm a soldier, but you bring something into war that doesn't belong in it. You trick men into death with your body.
> X-27: Give me a kiss.
> Kranau: You're a cheat and a liar.
> X-27: Why don't you stay here? Perhaps I don't always cheat and lie.
> Kranau: If you kept me here another minute, I'd not only be in danger of losing my life, but of falling in love with you, you devil.

Kranau's naive distinction between his brand of deception and X-27's hinges on his self-identification as a soldier, a narrow view already challenged by Sternberg's expressed distrust of the uniform.

X-27 at gambling casino in satin lamé (with Victor McLaglen as Lieutenant Kranau). (Photofest)

It is more fully refined later through redefinition in the film's final scene.

X-27's next assignment is to obtain information regarding the position and planned offensive of the enemy. She travels to her destination in the garb of an aviator, but once there, she assumes a role quite unlike any that Dietrich has played thus far in her career. Dressed as a peasant scrubwoman, in dirndl skirt and boots, and wearing no makeup, Dietrich is surprisingly de-glamorized, and the result is startling to the viewer who has associated her, even in her streetwalker clothes, with exceptional beauty and irresistible charisma.

X-27 disguised as a peasant woman (with Kranau). (Museum of Modern Art Film Stills Archive)

Raymond Durgnat, writing as O. O. Green, commented on the love with which Sternberg made her into a Russian peasant "with a pale, bulbous face, like potatoes, acquiring a fascinating near-ugliness and a clumsy vitality."[12] The unusual treatment here, accentuated by Sternberg's flat, uncharacteristic lighting, creates what Richard Dyer terms a "problematic fit" between star image and film character. Dyer suggests that in certain instances, a contradiction may exist between the star's image and the character as constructed, causing a contradiction or disjuncture in the film's textual system.[13] Here, the problematic fit serves Sternberg's purposes, however. The playfulness of this characterization—Dietrich's feigned coyness, her teasing temptation of the lecherous Russian colonel, the slapstick comedy of the pursuit around the colonel's room—and its contextual identification as calculated disguise or masquerade actually support Sternberg's strategy to maintain Dietrich's elusiveness and viewer distance while challenging character credibility. Dyer suggests that if we are to deem the film successful, character construction should not be visible, and characters should have credible lives of their own.[14] By making us aware of role-playing within this film's narrative, Sternberg makes us correspondingly aware of its falseness in the construction of a film. Sternberg made the same self-reflexive directorial gesture in earlier films such as *The Last Command, Blonde Venus* and *Shanghai Express.* As Durgnat suggests, "there are as many Marlenes in this film as there are Alec Guinnesses in an Ealing comedy."[15] Deception is at the core of *Dishonored,* and this thematic scheme stresses character duality. Disguise thereby becomes a signifier of actor/star/character layering, and Sternberg's playful treatment of it an exposure of the distinction between actor/star and character. While it is true, as Leo Braudy suggests, that sound films can explore the tension between the "real" person playing the role and the image projected on the screen[16] (Dyer's "problematic fit"), Sternberg highlights that tension with a playfulness that communicates his understanding. The end result is a more elusive Dietrich. In the rift between actor/star and character, the illusion presented by role-playing is eliminated and the star, with her secret self, remains always just beyond our grasp.

The use of the peasant costume as signifier of actor/star/character layering is further supported by costume gesture and dialogue. After obtaining secret information from the drunk, unconscious Colonel Korvin, X-27 is captured while trying to escape. Kranau confronts her and their ensuing dialogue serves to highlight the tension between concealment (signified by layering) and revelation (signified by costume).

> Kranau: I like your masquerade. . . . I'm sorry, I'll have to search you, X-27. Take your things off . . .
> X-27: Shall I go on with my undressing?

As X-27 peels away layers of costume (shawl, jacket, overskirt), the gesture's erotic appeal notwithstanding, the metaphor is unmistakably familiar, and one to which Sternberg referred again in *Blonde*

Venus; undressing, or the removal of layers, becomes a signifier of discovery, and is opposed to layering, which frustrates it.

Sternberg's discomfort with Kranau's earlier-stated double standard becomes more overt in the director's investigation of character reversal and duality through both dialogue and visual cues. X-27's statement is almost a direct repetition of a line delivered earlier by Kranau when he spoke of how important it would be for X-27 to capture him. He had said, "This would have been quite a feather in your cap, wouldn't it?" X-27 now says, "This is quite a feather in your cap, isn't it?"

The verbal similarity suggests character crossover, whereby one character exchanges places with another. The duality is further highlighted by images of X-27 and Kranau reflected in a mirror, reinforcing Sternberg's questioning of Kranau's double standard. But Kranau's response reflects his ambivalence: he is intrigued and seduced by the trickery he has previously accused her of.

> Kranau: The more you cheat and the more you lie, the more exciting you become, X-27.

Kranau's conflict metaphorically describes the film experience. Aware as we are of its falseness, its deception, we are nonetheless seduced by its illusions.

In the next scene, a typical Hollywood follow-up to the unshown sex act, Kranau is also in peasant garb, a change which suggests the dropping of defenses as well as the similarity of character. Kranau is tricked into drinking a drug-laced cocktail, allowing X-27 to escape once again.

The next scene presents X-27 in a leather version of the well-known spy trenchcoat. It is in this scene that she makes her first choice between love and patriotism, deciding not to reveal Kranau's identity to his Austrian captors. When she realizes that he is close to being discovered, she convinces the Austrian questioners to allow her to try her luck with extracting information. During their dramatically lit private moments together, X-27 "accidentally" drops her pistol; it is retrieved by Kranau, who then escapes. She is tried for treason and sentenced to execution. Visited by a priest who asks for her last request, X-27 (now dressed in prison clothes) asks to die in a uniform of her own choosing:

> Priest: What would you call a uniform of your own choosing?
> X-27: Any dress I wore when I served my countrymen, instead of my country.
> Priest: I will send for your clothes.

X-27 in her "spy" trenchcoat (with Kranau). (Museum of Modern Art Film Stills Archive)

Her uniform turns out to be the costume of the streetwalker, an outfit we have seen in the scene in which Dietrich was first enlisted as a spy. As reported by David Chierichetti:

Sternberg directed Banton to come up with something bizarre for the final scenes of *Dishonored*, for Banton produced a riot of contrasting textures that only Dietrich's personality and carriage could support. She wore a coat with an enormous trimming of monkey fur at the collar and cuffs, a small hat entirely covered in feathers, with a long black veil with white dots and a frilly lace jabot.[17]

Chierichetti fails to point out that the costume was used earlier in the film. Its repetition in the film's last scene emphasizes Sternberg's recognition of the streetwalker's costume as a uniform, and prepares for that costume's redefinition. X-27 uses an officer's sword as a mirror to adjust her hat and veil, and walks bravely out to the waiting firing squad. While a young officer breaks down, refusing to give orders to shoot her, Dietrich calmly applies lipstick and fixes her stockings, the latter action reminiscent of the film's opening gesture. The officer's remarks and her nonchalance highlight Sternberg's re-definition of the uniform:

> Officer: I will not kill a woman. I will not kill any more men either. You call this war; I call it butchery. You call this serving your country; you call this patriotism. I call it murder!

The officer's renunciation of soldiering, war, and patriotism is Sternberg's direct commentary on and exposure of traditional military/political values. As Andrew Sarris has suggested:

> His political males strut about in their ridiculous costumes . . . and then pass judgment on the only life-giving force in their midst. Yet it is Dietrich who ultimately passes judgment by choosing to die as a woman without a cause in a picture without a moral.[18]

Sarris' last sentence is self-contradictory, for Dietrich's cause *is* the exercise of her choice, and Sternberg's moral lies in allowing her to pass judgment on the state. By exposing the values of men at war and permitting X-27 to die in the uniform of her choice, Sternberg has redefined both the uniform and the notion of honor, while re-evaluating the importance of romantic love.

Since the male uniform has already been discredited through its association with treason and deception, X-27's "uniform" remains the one that is most honest about its intentions. Throughout all of her disguises, she has never denied who she is, nor lost her sense of purpose. While her outer identities have changed, her inner reality and self-awareness have remained constant, and she has always understood the power of her own beauty. She faces death as she has faced her men—all of them customers—and the adjustment of her costume and makeup, reminiscent of the first scene, indicate her consistency of purpose. Always faithful to her nature as a woman, she dies, as Andrew Sarris has indicated, "for matters of sex rather than state."[19] It is not surprising, therefore, that Sternberg would have been disturbed by the film's title; however, its contrast with the film's point of view creates a kind of Sternbergian irony that questions surface appearances.

Dishonored is the first of several Sternberg films to utilize disguise as a central costume sign for deception. In his next film, *An American Tragedy,* a project Sternberg accepted while waiting for Dietrich to return from a vacation in Europe, the director was attracted to the idea of deception inherent in Dreiser's original novel. But without

Dietrich as vehicle for Banton's costumes, or the Dietrich persona to signify duality or the dichotomous woman, the film seems far less attentive to costume signs, and it is not until *Shanghai Express* that Sternberg would return to his emphasis upon costume as a metaphor for disguise. *Dishonored* defined deception as both sexual and political, using disguise to conceal both forms of deceit. (Later in his career, Sternberg would return to these themes, treating them comically in *Jet Pilot* and *The King Steps Out*.) *Shanghai Express* defines deception in more exclusively sexual terms, placing even greater emphasis on emotional loyalty and sacrifice without political context.

Shanghai Express (1932) gave Sternberg an opportunity to exercise his increasing awareness of decor, photography, sound and acting. It was to be his last joint effort with cinematographer Lee Garmes; they had worked together on *Morocco*, *Dishonored* and *An American Tragedy*, and Garmes had proven to be extremely helpful in translating Sternberg's personal vision to the screen.[20] *Shanghai Express*, more than any of Sternberg's previous efforts, stresses the exotic through an obsessive concern for visual detail—detail which, in its richness and depth, paradoxically creates not a more realistic world but a less accessible one.

Atmosphere and location are established immediately. Behind the opening credits a huge gong containing Chinese characters is struck as other characters are drawn onto a page, signaling the importance of decor[21] and the indecipherability of appearances. Smoke wafting into the image obscures a frame already crowded with titles and flowers. Sternberg's usual visual clutter is immediately evident in the multiplaned mise-en-scène of his opening shots: the background train, peopled with passengers; the middle-ground signs of locale, establishing place with cages, nets and umbrellas constantly obscuring the view; and the movement of people in the foreground. These people remain unidentified—they are shot from the waist down—and their movements are intensified by the relentlessly mobile camera and dizzying dissolves, all creating a chaotic and visually confusing scene. The confusion continues in Sternberg's use of window frames, shades and character compartmentalization. After Lily is initially introduced, her character is built, in part, by reputation and rumor. As men describe her notoriety, Lily (Dietrich) is shown inside her compartment, pulling down a window shade and hiding herself from view. It is a masterful aural/visual clue to the film's ensuing pattern of tension between appearance and reality, spectacle and concealment; the juxtaposition of image and sound suggests that what one hears may not always present a complete or accurate picture.

Lily's first outfit introduces the tension between concealment and spectacle. She is initially seen, only with great difficulty, in the back seat of a dimly lit taxicab, but as she emerges into the sunlight, her richly feathered costume and veiled hat take over the role played earlier by Sternberg's mise-en-scène; they obscure, even in close-up, the remarkable face of Dietrich, while suggesting the enigma of her character.

According to Joyce Rheuben, Sternberg is the cinema's biggest tease, presenting a vision of Dietrich while also obscuring her image behind veils, nets, hats and other obstructions.[22]

Lily's first outfit, while obscuring the true character of the woman beneath it, presents an immediately identifiable, however unreliable, image to both viewer and passenger. From her outfit she is instantly recognized as the "notorious white flower of China," the coaster who has "wrecked a dozen men up and down the China coast."

Recognition of her notorious identity is also made possible by her difference: she is white, blonde, and spectacularly beautiful. Blondness causes Lily to stand out in relief from the darker, more sensual woman in the film—the character of Hui Fei, played by Anna May Wong. In fact, if blondness is, as Maureen Turim has suggested, "a cultural fetish of white racist society,"[23] then Hui Fei's otherness is further highlighted by such a contrast. Fair hair has held its place in the European ideal of feminine beauty, "with fair-haired women often the object of the European male's desire."[24] While in literature, the dark-haired woman has traditionally been the more sensual, the more evil, in Greek mythology the sirens and mermaids, so fatal to men, had long, fair hair. Alfred Hitchcock exploded the myth of the fair-haired, innocent virgin in many of his films (most notably *Vertigo* and *Marnie*) and Longfellow seemed to express concern over its lack of innocence:

> Often treachery lies
> Underneath the fairest hair[25]

It is not surprising, then, to see Sternberg's siren transformed to a blonde (she had been a brunette in her two previous films with Sternberg), a style which was becoming more popular with the rise of such stars as Mae West, Jean Harlow and Carole Lombard.

Lily's first outfit, layered with feathers and beads, with her face half-hidden behind a veil, introduces her as the femme fatale.[26] Sternberg, in the tradition of artists who presented the femme fatale, often connected beauty with danger,[27] and here it is the Black Swan that represents the dark, tempestuous, deceptive side of Lily's nature.

Dietrich as Shanghai Lily, covered in cock-feathers in *Shanghai Express*. (Movie Star News)

Swan Lake, undoubtedly a major influence on this first outfit, is an appropriate source. It too deals with such Sternbergian concerns as disguise, deception and the nature of true love. The Swan queen Odette, under the spell of a magician, falls in love with Siegfried, and explains to him that the magician's spell can be broken only if a man remains faithful to her. It is a love test not dissimilar to that imposed upon each other by Lily and Lieutenant Harvey:

> Lily: When I needed your faith, you withheld it. And now, when I don't need it and don't deserve it, you give it to me!

The element of deception through disguise is introduced when Siegfried meets Odile, the magician's daughter, disguised as Odette. The famous Black Swan pas de deux, in which Odile attempts to convince Siegfried that she is Odette, is a scene which Sternberg recreates in a verbal pas de deux. There is an exchange of queries between Lily and Harvey during their first encounter on the train; it emphasizes Harvey's attempt to uncover Lily's true identity by contrasting her present image with his memory of her, while commenting on her transformation.

> Lily: You haven't changed at all, Doctor.
> Harvey: Well! You've changed a lot, Magdalen.

Dietrich's character has changed, at least superficially, in her transformation from Magdalen to Lily, but her inner qualities of faithfulness and loyalty, symbolized by the immutable photograph of her that Harvey carries in his watch, are still present. They will later be made evident, not only by actions, but also by costume, when she becomes the Mary Magdalene her Christian name implies. In fact, her reference to the one thing she would have changed, i.e., the length of her hair ("I wouldn't have bobbed my hair"), has significance in light of historical associations with hair length. As Allison Lurie has noted, long hair has traditionally been associated with sexual women. Mary Magdalene in Christian art, for example, is usually depicted with hair that touches her feet.[28] Lily's regret suggests a desire to maintain a spiritual, physical connection with the biblical character with whom she is associated.

Names, too, reflect change and deception, and Lily makes reference to the fact that it has taken "more than one man to change my name to Shanghai Lily." Harvey reiterates that he "hasn't changed at all," a verbal expression of his own moral and emotional rigor.

Change is often literalized by Sternberg through costume or costume gestures (e.g., change of costume, costume alteration by addition or subtraction of an accessory, striptease). Characters who can change their costume or their names are characters who may not be trustworthy. Lily's change back to Magdalen, effected by an act of intense prayer and a switch in costume to puritanical dress, saves Harvey from being blinded by the vindictive rebel leader, Chang. Her change is clearly motivated by love and self-sacrifice. Later, Chang changes costumes from civilian to soldier when his identity as rebel leader is revealed. His change is threatening and dangerous. Change, for Sternberg, is ultimately ironic, since it exists only as part of the endless circle of desire which leads either nowhere, or back to itself.

Impressions change as rapidly as does costume, and are often used to further emphasize moral rigor. The obstinate Reverend Carmichael changes his opinion of Shanghai Lily from outrage at her immorality to admiration of her faith after he observes her praying for Harvey. His understanding that "love without faith, like religion without faith, doesn't amount to very much," expresses his new identification with Lily's religiosity. When Harvey questions Carmichael's "faith" in what Lily says, the missionary expresses Harvey's major conflict.

> Carmichael: I know you men of science regard me and my kind as meddlesome fanatics, but I'd rather have one grain of my faith than all your scientific disbelief.

Skepticism and scientific disbelief are analogues for lack of faith, the unemotional distancing of self for the purpose of objective analysis. According to John Belton, Sternberg values the extremes of science and faith as mutually exclusive poles between which his characters fluctuate. Unlike Frank Borzage, who is more interested in the extreme of faith, Sternberg finds the middle ground most fascinating to explore.[29]

Lily herself notes her own "transformation" when initially approached by Chang, who requests that she go away with him:

> Chang: I had no reason to believe my invitation would give offense to Shanghai Lily.
> Lily: Shanghai Lily has reformed.
> Chang: You don't mean to say that the eloquence of Dr. Carmichael has worked this miracle? Or is Captain Harvey to be credited with this extraordinary change?
> Lily: Maybe.

In her rejection of Chang, she exercises the choice of which she has always been capable, surprising those who consider her undiscriminating. She is dressed here in the characteristic puritanical dress which marks her transformation to the good woman/Madonna.

Lily as Madonna. (Jerry Ohlinger)

Sternberg's dangerous women are most often dressed in black, a color associated with the "black widow spider, black cat or . . . death itself."[30]

Hollywood vamp black was doubtless inspired as much by the possibilities of black-and-white cinematography as by the conventions of the romantic femme fatale. As movies continued to influence glamour, color became less associated with elegance and was replaced by the black and white spectrum of sensual textures: sequins, net and lace that had their own sexual significance.[31]

Anne Hollander suggests that the symbolism of black as a clothing color has been stronger, historically, than that of any other color, including white, because of black's association with the sinister.

While black calls up fears of the darkness of night and even death, it is still attractive.[32] Hollander distinguishes between the use of black as a rebellious antifashion which seeks to isolate and dramatize the wearer, and the use of black as an expression of sobriety and self-denial. In fact, Sternberg utilizes black in both forms to express Lily's dichotomous character. Her first cock-feathered outfit as Shanghai Lily serves to isolate and distinguish her in a sea of greys, while the sober, puritanical, white-collared black dress she wears for her prayer for Harvey's safety suggests her transformation to self-sacrificing Madonna. This black dress, expressing calm and sobriety, is also reflective of the fashion for black which followed the wild period of 'twenties clothing.[33]

Disguise is the costume sign which serves as organizational principle for *Shanghai Express*. Sternberg uses disguise as the visual analogue to themes of appearance/reality, faith/distrust, understanding/blindness and character ambiguity. Almost all of the travelers on board the Shanghai Express are in some form of disguise, or are concealing something.[34] Mrs. Haggerty, who runs a respectable boarding house, has violated the train's rule prohibiting animals in the passenger area by hiding her dog. It is found and placed in the baggage compartment. Mr. Baum, who poses as an invalid, is really an opium smuggler. Chang turns out to be the leader of the rebel forces, while Major Lenard, still in the uniform of the French army, reveals through questioning that he has actually been discharged. Sam Salt is a gambler who initially hides his jewelry and later admits it is fake. Reverend Carmichael sees Lily for what she is, despite being morally judgmental. And Captain Harvey is actually traveling to Shanghai in order to secretly perform surgery on a high government official. Here, Sternberg has created a complex series of first impressions which will later be revealed as false, exercising his control over cinema's tendency toward slow revelation. As John Baxter has suggested, "Sternberg takes malicious delight in peeling away the multiple masks that comprise personality."[35] Often, his characters' masks mislead, creating an impediment to cinematic disclosure.

In some cases, disguise is handled visually through costume. Baum "dresses" as an invalid; he is always wrapped in a blanket which supposedly protects him from dangerous drafts. Lenard's uniform disguises his disgrace; Lily's initial costume masks her humanity and depth of feeling; and Chang poses as a civilian to hide his association with the rebels. At one point, the image of Chang and Harvey, dressed exactly alike in short, white dinner jackets, expresses a bit of Sternbergian irony: while both men desire Lily, they differ in their approaches. Chang's direct, forceful use of a diabolical bargain to keep her with him ("His eyes for your body") contrasts sharply with Harvey's repressed desire.

Sternberg's control of information through his use of disguise is layered with meaning. A film costume is a form of deception, a middle layer of informational material which disguises the actor while engaging audience participation in the disguise. One might go to a Dietrich film to see Dietrich, but it is always Dietrich disguised as a particular character. Sternberg further complicates the disguise by presenting misinformation. He has, to use clothing sociologist Alison Lurie's terminology, learned to "lie in the language of dress," a language that communicates in many forms of dishonesty, including ambiguity, error, self-deception, misinterpretation and irony.[36]

Chang (Warner Oland) and Harvey (Clive Brook) in their military uniforms. (Museum of Modern Art Film Stills Archive)

In *Shanghai Express*, as in the earlier *Morocco* and *Dishonored*, Sternberg classifies Dietrich-as-soldier through acts of heroism, complemented here by costume and by gestures which relate to or foreground such costume. There are many uniforms in the film. Chang and Harvey wear uniforms to indicate their affiliation with the military; the uniform worn by Lenard, which hides his disgrace, throws doubt upon the authority and bravery with which the male military uniform is traditionally associated. Such doubt allows Sternberg to present his only real soldier, the woman whose actions reveal the kind of sacrifice and honor necessary to be a member of Sternberg's elite army. By offering to go away with Chang, Lily prevents Harvey from being blinded, a condition with which he is already, metaphorically afflicted, since he refuses to see her for what she is. Thus Lily sacrifices herself with a gesture that will save her lover. Sternberg highlights such actions with costume gestures. Earlier in the film, Harvey and Lily compare "medals":

Lily: New, isn't it?
Harvey: Yes.
Lily: Bravery?
Harvey: Of sorts . . . New? (as he looks at her brooch, pinned in the same position as his medals)
Lily: Yes.
Harvey: Very becoming.

Lily has won her medals for "skill" in a world in which a woman must live by her wits. Later, after kissing Harvey, she removes his soldier's cap, tilts it rakishly on her head and pops it (a typical Sternberg/Dietrich gesture) to challenge his rigid, military values which require fidelity even through final separation.

Harvey: I wish you could tell me there'd been no other men.
Lily: I wish I could, Doc, but five years in China is a long time.

Here, according to Molly Haskell, she assumes male military attire "not to discredit the male sex, but to challenge the system of values by which it puffs itself up with false pride and vainglory."[37]

Chang recognizes Lily's soldierly code of honor when she promises to stay with him in exchange for Harvey's eyesight.

Chang: A man is a fool to trust any woman, but I believe a word of honor would mean something to you.

Again, Sternberg alters the image of the apparent femme fatale by presenting her, not as the devious woman she appears to be, but as a woman of her word, and one who deserves the salute of her fellow soldiers.[38]

Lily wearing Harvey's cap. (Movie Star News)

Costume gesture is a source of thematic information for Sternberg. At the end of the film, Lily buys Harvey a new watch, this one without the immutable photograph. Harvey accepts the watch, as he accepts Lily: he begs for another chance and promises that he'll be different. As they embrace, he is still holding his whip and glove, and after a dissolve to the crowded train station, an unseen transfer of whip and glove from Harvey's hand to Lily's occurs as she drops both accessories behind his back. It is a triumphant gesture, symbolizing her role in the discarding of his rigidity and the breakdown of his narrowly defined military value system.

Another favorite Sternberg attempt to control cinema's tendency to reveal information rests in his anti-Bazinian approach. As mentioned earlier, Peter Wollen has suggested that in opposing any kind of realism, Sternberg attempted to destroy the bond between the natural world and the film image.[39] In creating his own personal heterocosm, Sternberg was often attracted to the exotic. A thirties film audience was not likely to care about verisimilitude of detail in either decor or costume when familiarity with locale or culture was so infrequent. This allowed the costume and set designers more freedom to exaggerate details of style.[40]

Characters and actors can also convey exotica, and foreignness can be manifest in both. Dietrich, like Garbo, "looked" different, and even an attempt to Americanize her appeal through rigorous diet did not camouflage her foreignness. Although her English improved throughout her career, Dietrich would always sound different.

Oriental women, like Oriental locations, were inherently exotic and mysterious, and sets and costumes were specifically made to enhance these elements.[41] Anna May Wong was the exception to the rule that true Orientals were relegated to bit parts in Hollywood films. Wong was a full-blooded Chinese who was able to portray both extremes of Oriental stereotypes: she played the sensual dragon lady and the shy geisha with equal credibility, and often transcended the usual exploitation of the exotic Oriental as mere showcase for spectacular costumes.[42] In *Shanghai Express,* Sternberg rounds out the two-dimensional stereotype by making Hui Fei a woman of complexity as well as a woman of mystery and exoticism. She is immediately responded to on the basis of her "looks." Reverend Carmichael's declaration that he hasn't "lived in this country for ten years not to know a woman like that when I see one," suggests a superficial judgment based on physical appearance. It may be a touch of Sternbergian ironic wit to suggest that such immediate recognition signals a familiarity which may breed more contempt than the missionary is willing to admit. Though as a missionary, Carmichael's redemption of lost souls might have brought him into contact with such women, Sternberg's joke remains ambiguous. Sternberg expresses his refusal to judge Hui Fei's morality by allowing her a sense of outrage and violation toward Chang, and by making her the agent of revenge in killing him. In redeeming herself, Hui Fei also frees Lily, making her deed not only vengeful, but heroic as well.

As an analogue to the extreme visual clutter that crowded his frames, Sternberg cluttered his characters with costume accessories as a kind of camouflage. It is possible that Banton costumed Dietrich in veils primarily to obscure her "weaker" profile.[43] Baxter notes that "in all her films up to *Song of Songs,* Dietrich reveals only her right profile, the left side of her face always obscured by hair, furs or a shadow," and that Dietrich's nose was "awkwardly shaped."[44] It is even more likely, however, that Sternberg himself, based partly on his early jobs as apprentice in a millinery store and stock clerk in a lace warehouse, where he gained his knowledge of and liking for fabrics,[45] exploited the use of costume accessories as camouflage.

Hui Fei (Anna Mae Wong) and other "disguised" characters on board the Shanghai Express. (Jerry Ohlinger)

Veils are literal, if not metaphorical, impediments to discovery and display. Sternberg himself suggests that "the average human being lives behind an impenetrable veil and will disclose his deep emotions only in a crisis which robs him of control."[46] Veils, for Sternberg, become a recurring costume accessory suggestive of mystery, disguise, impenetrability. Veils also suggested romance and provided the designer with the challenge of utilizing an important costume detail without obscuring the face or detracting from character.[47]

While veils were clearly fashionable in the thirties and were added to make the wearer more attractive, their historical significance includes a variety of meanings, among them bondage, modesty, religious fervor, status and mourning.[48]

Lily's veil, however, seems to have a purpose that differs markedly from any of the above-mentioned historical signifiers. While it may camouflage an "imperfect" face, it is used primarily to obscure, to mystify, to control the amount of pleasure the viewer receives through contemplation. Even the close-up, the cinematic technique that normally permits and encourages scrutiny, is here rendered impossible by Sternberg's accessorial interference. In addition, the veil represents Lily's moral ambiguity in the same way that expressionistic lighting serves the imaginative purpose of Orson Welles, as his Kane moves in and out of shadow, always presenting the enigma, the puzzle that is never to be solved. As Alexander Walker states, the veil creates a visual contrast with the lower half of Lily's face, establishing the "chiarascuro of her sordid soul."[49]

Fur is used in *Shanghai Express* to enhance the photographic intensity of Dietrich's face as well as to signify power.[50] Lily's costume is trimmed in fur when she is most blatantly sexually aggressive. When she slowly and sensually brings Harvey's face down to meet hers in a kiss, she is wearing a huge, lush fur collar that frames her face. Historically, furs have been a signal of superiority for the wearer. Since they clearly represented the struggle between man and beast as well as the results of that struggle, furs became a popular form of even the most primitive ornament or costume.[51] Lily's achievement, i.e., the sexual and emotional power she has held over Harvey for the past five years, is signaled by her fur collar, worn proudly, like the mane of a lion, historically a trophy for the ancient Egyptians.[52]

Gloves are carefully designed and chosen to complement and accessorize Dietrich's total look, but again, their significance in history and culture may bear a relationship to costume gesture in the film. Historically, gloves were carried by lovers as a sign of devotion or hurled to the ground to challenge a rival.[53] When Lily drops Harvey's glove behind his back in the film's last scene, the suggestion is that their sexual rivalry, along with his resistance and rigor, will be abandoned to desire and mutual love.

Shanghai Express may be Sternberg's most complete excursion into the potentially rich world of exotic costume signification. While the exotic still fascinates him in films such as *The Shanghai Gesture* and *Macao*, the attention in these later films, due to the dissolution of his association with Dietrich, focuses less on the star as the carrier of costume signs and more on the city as it functions as a metaphor for exoticism and inaccessibility. In its use of disguise as a metaphor for the inaccessibility of the cinematic image, *Shanghai Express* echoes concerns expressed in *Dishonored,* while it prefigures comedies such as *Jet Pilot* and *The King Steps Out.*

The King Steps Out (1936), Sternberg's second film in a two-picture contract with Columbia (the first was *Crime and Punishment,* 1935), has been summarily dismissed by critics as well as by the director himself as an uncharacteristic Sternberg work. Andrew

Sarris believed that it hardly deserved any detailed analysis, noting
its failure "even as an exercise in style."[54] Sternberg suggested that
both Columbia assignments merely carried his name and little else.[55]
While the film differs markedly from most other Sternberg efforts
in visual style (Sarris called it Sternberg's "whitest film in terms of
visual texture"[56]) and subject matter (it is Sternberg's only musical),
The King Steps Out contains some familiar signs of Sternberg's art.
Particularly interesting are its references to costume signs as they
relate to deception and period, placing *The King Steps Out* among
those Sternberg works which deal with similar issues (*Dishonored,
Shanghai Express* and *Jet Pilot* deal with deception and disguise,
while *The Scarlet Empress* approaches period through costume
signs).

The narrative concerns a vivacious young princess named Cissie
(Grace Moore), who tries to prevent the forced marriage of her sister
to the Emperor Franz Josef (Franchot Tone) of Austria. Disguised
as a dressmaker, Cissie seduces the young emperor, falling in love
with him herself, and permitting her sister to marry the man she
really loves (Victor Jory). There are numerous other disguises
throughout the film, including that of Cissie's father, the Duke (Walter Connolly), who prefers to spend his time in the forest disguised
as a Bavarian woodsman, or at inns downing steins of beer. The
emperor also participates in the sartorial deception when, disguised
as an infantry officer, he goes among his people to attend his own
birthday celebration. The film concludes with the revelation of
everyone's true identity and the usual happily-ever-after Hollywood
ending.

Besides the motifs of disguise and deception which run throughout
the film there is the familiar Sternberg festival, or carnival, presented
here as a birthday celebration for the emperor. Here, as in all of
Sternberg's prior festivals, characters in disguise sweep through
spaces cluttered with signs of merrymaking, creating a dreamlike
atmosphere for the discovery of mutual passion. As Marcel Oms
suggests, Sternberg's festivals function as imagination, representing
the delirium of liberated energy which often serves to clarify the
search for self.[57]

The film's unspecified period (the Hapsburgs ruled Austria from
1276 to 1918) and the frivolity of the musical genre probably permitted Sternberg and his costume designer, Ernest Dryden, greater lib-
erty and the styles appear to cover several periods, ranging from
1855 to 1897. Cissie's dresses are a mélange of late nineteenth-cen-
tury fashions, combining 1876 jacket bodices with 1860 skirts and a
series of hats that range from 1865 to 1893. Her sleeves, slightly

enlarged at the top of the shoulder, did not appear until 1897. Other women are more consistent in their dress, following the style of Cissie's 1860 skirt. Men are more difficult to place historically, since most wear uniforms. Once again, Sternberg makes reference to the importance of the uniform in establishing identity and self-importance. Cissie's father refuses to wear his uniform until he is forced to do so in order to free his daughter from prison, while the emperor wears the uniform of an infantryman in order to hide his true identity. Actually, Sternberg parodies his own former references to uniform by suggesting that both men use it to hide an identity they do not wish to reveal: the Duke dislikes his identification with the uniform, a discomfort visible in the difficulty he has with its feathered hat, which practically chokes him, while the Emperor hides behind his uniform.

There are many stripes, plaids and polka dots among the fabric patterns, and while there is some evidence for their historical existence, they have been used here in abundance to "musicalize" the general look of the film. Since black-and-white film lacks the opportunity for fantasy that color film has, with its "pastel potential," one way to maintain a look of fantasy was with fabric texture and pattern. Excessive stripes, plaids and polka dots, as well as shiny taffetas and satins, provide a sparkle that compensates for lack of color and suits the more frivolous look of the musical.

The playing with period in *The King Steps Out* becomes even more interesting when seen in relationship to Sternberg's other major period film, *The Scarlet Empress*. In its approach to period, its attention to deception-through-disguise, and in details of plot (i.e., the uncomfortable journey; the importance of social climbing; the meetings between Cissie and Franz Josef compared to those between Sophia and Peter), *The King Steps Out* borrows from *The Scarlet Empress*.[58] In fact, the former film, like *Jet Pilot*, is a comic inversion of Sternberg's more sober approaches to similar themes. Self-parody appears to have been Sternberg's method of asserting some degree of control over material that the director did not consider his own.[59]

The King Steps Out, despite Sternberg's repudiation of the film (John Baxter reports that it was a film he requested be excluded from retrospectives of his work[60]), exemplifies the director's struggle to maintain control over all aspects of creativity. In its approach to important concerns of other films (i.e., deception, disguise, period) and in its attention to questions surrounding the nature of the medium, *The King Steps Out* is clearly a Sternberg work.

Among the films over which Sternberg exercised scant control, *Jet*

Cissie (Grace Moore) in a mélange of prints and plaids in *The King Steps Out*. (Photofest)

Pilot still manages to emerge with subtle reminders of the director's golden age. Typical Sternbergian concerns such as deception, spying and disguise form the structural basis for the film, a kind of comic inversion of the director's more serious approach used in both *Dishonored* and *Shanghai Express*.

In 1949, after two years of travel, Sternberg was approached by his former screenwriting collaborator, Jules Furthman, to make a film for Howard Hughes at RKO. Hughes wanted each prospective director to audition for the job by making a test sequence. Sternberg was able to justify the trial as a Hughes idiosyncrasy, rather than as a doubt about his talent,[61] and he shot a test, filming what he claims was one-sixth of the film in two days.[62] He signed a contract with Hughes to make two films, the second of which would be *Macao*.[63]

Sternberg seemed resigned to the restrictions of mere mechanical translation from script to screen, indicating that, initially, he had almost no freedom at all on the picture.[64] After shooting began, Sternberg had more autonomy than he had anticipated, although his progress was carefully monitored throughout the project.[65]

The editing process appears to have provided Sternberg with more control (he claims that no one interfered with him during the editing), but he still considered the project one in which he was only one of many participants and considered his functions "shadowy."[66]

Editing was not completed until 1953 and producer Furthman worried that the film's fashions and flying scenes would appear dated. Hughes, considering the film incomplete, refused to release it; however, after he sold RKO in 1955, the film was prepared for release by a team that recut and reshot it, as well as updated it with more contemporary flying sequences.[67]

In an interview with Peter Bogdanovich, Sternberg succinctly summarized his feelings about the assignment.

Bogdanovich: You planned *Jet Pilot* as a satire on the jet age, didn't you?
Sternberg: I just followed instructions.[68]

Despite his renunciation of the film, *Jet Pilot* is one of those "assignments" which retains some familiar signs of Sternberg's earlier art. Its central theme, i.e., deception/spying, is reminiscent of *Dishonored*, as are its concerns with the dichotomous woman, the untrustworthy "Mata Hari," played here by Janet Leigh. In addition, with the help of RKO designer Michael Woulfe, Sternberg returns to costume as a stylistic expression of narrative and thematic concerns.

Because of the severe restrictions placed upon him, including the reshooting and reediting of the film, it is difficult to classify *Jet Pilot* as a uniquely Sternbergian work; however, what remains in the final print bears enough resemblance to earlier films to consider it part of Sternberg's oeuvre, and its attention to costume signs warrants investigation.

Jet Pilot deals with the efforts of a disguised political refugee, actually a Russian spy named Anna (Janet Leigh), to extract secret information regarding air force planes from an American colonel (John Wayne) she is assigned to seduce. After a series of deceptions planned by each of the characters (Wayne's character, Colonel Shannon, also wants information on Russian planes), the two fall in love and decide to marry in order to prevent Anna's deportation to Russia. When Shannon returns with her to Russia, he knows that she is a spy offering only useless information to the Soviets. She begins to find Russian sparseness difficult to swallow in contrast to juicy capitalist steaks and Palm Beach vacations. To prevent Shannon from being brainwashed and rendered a zombie by Soviet officials, Anna steals a plane and the lovers return to America.

In its narrative and thematic design, *Jet Pilot* appears to be a comic inversion of *Dishonored*. Both films are centrally concerned with deception and spying, and touch on issues of sexual misconception, soldierly honor and the untrustworthy woman. The film begins with a joke based on sexual misconception, a comic salute to the cross-dressing and sexual disguise of *Morocco* and *Blonde Venus*. While in pursuit of a Russian jet, American flyers assume that its pilot is a man. Anna emerges from the cockpit in a sparkling white aviator's suit, noticeably nipped in at the waist, but it is not until she removes her helmet that the men realize their mistake. Exclamations of "A woman!" "A lady!" "A dame!" convey their surprise. The men's surprise seems a humorous commentary on spectatorial response to a woman in drag, and we are reminded of the fact that Dietrich fooled no one with her sexual masquerade in other films.

Anna immediately asks to be treated as an officer and not as a woman, a distinction Sternberg made in films that redefined honor (*Dishonored* and *Shanghai Express*). But it is a request she really does not mean, since, following this scene, she willingly removes her clothes in order to be searched by the already suspicious Shannon. Since Shannon has been characterized as "one of those men who suspects everything he can't understand," it seems appropriate for Anna's ensuing striptease to be both, in her view, seductive (under her control) and, in his view, potentially revealing (under his control). Once again, Sternberg turns to the striptease to explore cinematic tensions. The removal of costume serves Anna's purpose (the promise of more) while thwarting Shannon's desire (to know, to see,

Anna (Janet Leigh) in her white aviator's suit from *Jet Pilot* (with Josef von Sternberg). (Photofest)

to have revealed) and the comic striptease is punctuated by roars of
jet engines that serve as amusing aural exclamation points.

It is also important to note that Anna is using her womanhood as
a kind of disguise to conceal her true identity as a spy, the striptease
serving as a comic inversion of the more traditional forms of disguise
that conceal identity. Sternberg is using sartorial layering whereby
the uniform disguises her womanhood and the striptease disguises
her real motives in order to present the idea of the deceptive woman.
Later in the film, Anna's duality is highlighted by the opposition of
Olga-the-spy to Anna-the-woman. Shannon, whose earlier recognition of her duality has substantiated his distrust, originally makes
this distinction and it plays an important role later on in the film.
Following Shannon's discovery of Anna's deception, he expresses his
disappointment by highlighting her duality.

> Shannon: I see you as two girls: Anna, the lovely kid I thought was à
> refugee, and Olga, that Soviet tootsie roll who made a chump outa
> me.

But her very duality saves his life when later, as he flies a jet after
having been drugged by a new Soviet commanding officer, Anna
follows him in another plane. In an effort to convince him of her
loyalty and love, she signals him via radio.

> Leigh: This isn't Olga—this is Anna! Repeat—this is Anna!

Her distinction between woman-as-spy and woman-as-lover reinforces notions of duality while redefining the concept of honor.
Clearly, woman must choose between the honor of serving her country and the honor of serving her lover, and Sternberg supports the
latter, just as he did in the more serious *Dishonored.* While *Jet Pilot*
appears to be another typical anti-Communist tract, both popular
and required during Hollywood's cold war paranoia, Sternberg's
ideology is extremely superficial. In fact, his distinction between
communism and capitalism is signified more by the conflict between
luxury and scarcity (a conflict whose comic potential was explored
by Ernst Lubitsch in the 1939 film, *Ninotchka*) than by the more
serious conflict between good and evil depicted in most anti-Communist films of the cold war period. Here, Sternberg uses costume
and food to represent capitalist appetite. Sumptuous costume ensem-
bles and juicy steaks present irresistible alternatives to Soviet auster-
ity. In one scene in a shop, Anna admires a two-piece bathing suit.
Her statement that "capitalism has certain dangerous advantages" is

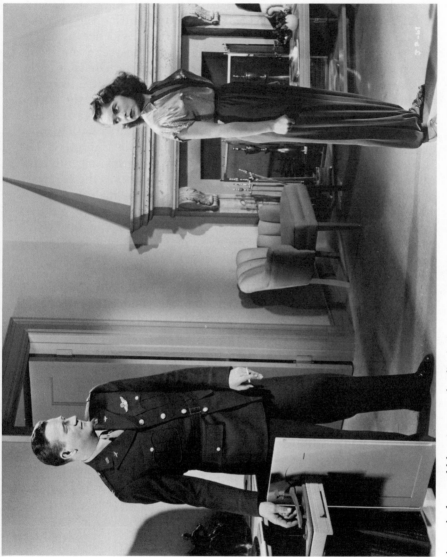

Anna in her gold lamé top and split genie pants (with John Wayne as Shannon). (Photofest)

answered by Wayne's political playfulness and Sternberg's sartorial
joke which uses costume as a metaphor: "One thing we have in
common with the Soviets: we both believe in uplifting the masses."

Numerous other costume references serve as evidence of Sternberg's interest in costume as an element of mise-en-scène, and while
the specifics of signification are not as rich as in the Dietrich cycle,
the attention to costume signs suggests Sternberg's contributions to
the project. Anna's gold lamé top and red genie pants, slit up the
sides, hint at revelation and are reminiscent of the semirevealing costumes in *The Blue Angel*. A Palm Beach shop cluttered with manne-
quins displaying cruise wear recalls the immobile statues of *The
Scarlet Empress*. The androgynous Russian uniform that authenticates Anna's "official" identity as Olga-the-spy evokes the prior use
of seductive costume and the striptease to attract the male in *Morocco*
and *Blonde Venus*. There are also numerous costume gestures
throughout the film, including Wayne's placement of a hat on Leigh's
head and Leigh's jumping out of a window while Wayne is left holding onto her pants. As Luc Moullet suggested,

> He has lost none of his genius for costume (rather to the contrary; think
> of the golden blouse, the red trousers with the lightning fasteners on the
> sides, already anticipating the parachute-skirts of *Anatahan*); and he has
> achieved the genius of the cineaste.[69]

Interference and lack of control notwithstanding, *Jet Pilot* maintains many signs of Sternberg's art. While his influence was not
complete enough to approach the structural richness of earlier efforts, the film provides a fascinating look at a directorial presence
struggling to maintain its identity through the radical alteration of
reshooting and reediting.

5

Stylization as Distance: *Morocco* and *The Devil Is A Woman*

In both *Morocco* (1930) and *The Devil Is A Woman* (1935), Sternberg turns to stylization as a means of distancing. While his methods differ in each film (*Morocco* experiments with campy artifice while *The Devil Is A Woman* uses glamour and characterization), both emphasize Sternberg's awareness of his medium while encouraging a similar awareness in the viewer.

In his autobiography, Sternberg expressed his agony at the difficulty of artistic fulfillment in the creation of motion pictures, pointing out the difference between mere representation/reproduction and art.[1]

It is clear that Bazinian realism was a notion that did not appeal to Sternberg, and he was constantly challenged by a need to thwart naturalistic representation. His defiance took the form of virulent antirealism in every aspect of filmmaking. He created what Peter Wollen has described as a "completely artificial realm," depending primarily on the imagination of the artist.[2] Sternberg viewed his medium in terms of painting, describing the screen as a "white canvas onto which the images are thrown."[3] Rejecting, in his exercise of artistry, the Bazinian notion of the existential bond between the natural world and the film image, Sternberg created his own personal heterocosm,[4] a world filled with myth. In using constructed sets and carefully planned scripts; in "taking the star system to its ultimate limit with Marlene Dietrich" reveling in "hieratic masks and costumes";[5] in cluttering his sets with nets, veils and other masking elements—Sternberg became the ultimate antirealist.

Wollen's argument is endorsed by Jack Babuscio, who refers to Sternberg's films as "acts of arrogance" and sees Sternberg's style as a result of the director's need to impose himself on his material.[6] But Babuscio advances Wollen's argument a step further by identifying Sternberg's artistry of artifice as camp. Camp has affinities with exaggeration, extravagance, artifice, and the communication of this sensibility is often accomplished through costume. As Susan Sontag has stated:

> The hallmark of camp is the spirit of extravagance. Camp is a woman walking around in a dress made of three million feathers.[7]

In fact, Sternberg's excess and grandiosity, his "love of the unnatural,"[8] and his campiness seem a perfect mode of artistic expression for an antirealist who subordinates plot, character and cinematic realism to the demands of style. Babuscio suggests that

> [Sternberg's films] are also camp in that they reflect the director's ironic attitude toward his subject matter—a judgment which says . . . that the content is of interest only insofar as it remains susceptible to transformation by means of stylization.[9]

The notion of Sternberg's style as camp is extremely helpful in analyzing his use of costume. Clearly, costume, a surface element which reflects taste as well as standards, serves emblematically to present, conceal, disguise, alter or exaggerate realities.

Sontag's idea that "camp sees everything in quotation marks—it's not a lamp, but a 'lamp'; not a woman but a 'woman'"[10] also describes Sternberg's stylistic italicization of film content and character. And in identifying camp as a characteristically gay sensibility, Babuscio refers to its attention to costume.

> Camp aims to transform the ordinary into something more spectacular. In terms of style, it signifies performance rather than existence. Clothes, decor, for example, can be a means of asserting one's identity, as well as a form of justification in a society which denies one's essential validity.[11]

For Sternberg, costume becomes a means, not only of asserting the director's essential validity, his presence, his ultimate control, but also as a sign of the artifice of his own personal cinema, a foregrounding of its performance against the background of its existence. It is a method of punctuation, serving as quotation marks to character and identity.

More generally, camp is about incongruity and irony.[12] Incongruity works well in Sternberg's resistance strategy, since it is a notion that suggests the inappropriateness to which he was so attracted, an incompatibility that often took the form of extravagance and outrageousness. Additionally, incongruity serves as another expression of Sternberg's attention to the contrast between surface and underlying truth—a theme often expressed in costume signs throughout the Dietrich cycle.

The outrageousness of Sternberg's costumes has been commented on by several critics. Raymond Durgnat points out that criticizing a Sternberg film unavoidably involves one in the poetry and psychopathology of fashion,[13] and Herman Weinberg notes Sternberg's escalating obsession with costume, referring to it as the director's "clothes madness."[14]

His severest critics accused Sternberg of unremitting tastelessness. In *Vanity Fair* he was attacked for making Dietrich a "paramount slut," fixating on her "legs in silk and buttocks in lace";[15] while French cinema historians condemned him for making films in which Dietrich became "a mere clothes horse, laden with feathers and jewels."[16] Such critics failed to see how costume worked as part of Sternberg's schema.

If irony and incongruity are the subject matter of camp, then androgyny is one of its most significant manifestations. Babuscio indicates that the most common of incongruous contrasts is that between masculine and feminine,[17] and Sontag cites the androgyne as one of the great images of camp sensibility, locating incongruity in sexual reversal.[18]

For Sternberg, incongruity-as-camp surfaces in androgynous costume, i.e., cross-dressing, which occurs in *Blonde Venus, The Blue Angel, Dishonored,* and *The Scarlet Empress.* In *Morocco,* particularly, campy incongruity acts as a filmic second skin, a cloak that mystifies the audience and impedes realism. It is a structural principle for the film's narrative and thematic design, and a restatement of a favorite Sternberg theme. In highlighting difference, incongruity becomes another way of suggesting that things are not as they seem. Cross-dressing disguises one's sexual identity and presents an outer appearance that does not match the inner reality of one's sexual self.

Morocco begins in a typically exotic locale, foregrounding the idea of foreignness through costume and behavior. While military music and rhythms are heard on the soundtrack, the natives of the Moroccan city prepare to welcome their heroes. Dressed in the emblematic costume of the Arab, i.e., white burnouses, the natives prepare for the return of the foreign legionnaires, whose uniforms accommodate customary native dress in only one minor way: the caps (kepi) they wear contain a piece of fabric presumably added to protect them from sand and sun. Other than this minor detail, the soldiers are presented as foreigners, both in terms of their costume difference and in the way in which they are regarded and welcomed by the native men and women. The Foreign Legion itself has its own connotations of incongruity and dislocation, since it is an armed force comprised of European volunteers, many of whom have joined out of a sense of disconnection from their own society. Incongruity is further highlighted by Sternberg's introduction of the waiting women, some of whom lift their veils in a gesture of teasing accommodation and seduction. While the legionnaires are given orders about "behaving themselves" and "acting like gentlemen," Sternberg cuts to a shot of Arabs engaged in religious custom (kneeling and praying), again foregrounding incongruity and the difference between the two cultures. Legionnaire Tom Brown (Gary Cooper) flirts with an unveiled native woman, tossing a bracelet to her in a gesture that, for the first time, links the two cultures. Here, in the film's first scene, Sternberg has presented his major theme, i.e., incongruity, through a series of visual images that emphasize the central character's foreignness and dislocation, using costume to signify his concerns.

Morocco's second scene is concerned with another arrival, that of Amy Jolly (Marlene Dietrich). As she emerges from the darkness of Lee Garmes's misty mise-en-scène, she is immediately noticed by La Bessiere (Adolphe Menjou), who offers his assistance and his business card. Like some of the native women in the previous scene, Amy also wears a veil (this one European, however), but she does not lift hers, and the contrast to the earlier scene foregrounds her inaccessibility. Her dark costume, in contrast to the lighter costumes of the Arab passengers on the ship on which she has arrived conveys her foreignness. She is later described by the ship's captain as a "suicide passenger," a "one-way ticket" who never returns. She is also identified as a vaudeville actress, another of Sternberg's favorite professions (cf. *The Blue Angel, Blonde Venus, Macao*), since the performer acts as a vehicle for typical Sternbergian tensions centered around impersonation and display. Both La Bessiere and Amy Jolly are travelers, foreigners in an exotic locale, and Sternberg links them in this introduction. He will elaborate on this comparison throughout the film, a comparison that will act as a thread for the continuation of the theme of incongruity-as-camp. As Andrew Sarris has suggested, La Bessiere and Amy are analogues of each other and she is often presented, through their similar costumes, as a representation of the male who seeks to seduce her.[19] *Morocco's* next scene, the cabaret performance which introduces the foreign Amy to a rather difficult audience comprised of both natives and Europeans, is the scene which unites all thematic and character elements of the two earlier scenes, as well as develops the notion of incongruity-as-camp through costume signs.

Amy Jolly (Dietrich) as a one-way passenger in *Morocco*. (Photofest)

To advance the analogy between La Bessiere and Amy, Sternberg presents the French bachelor in black-tie and tails. He makes the rounds throughout the cabaret, and, with great charm and civility, greets people he has not seen for awhile. Later, Amy table-hops in much the same way, charming various members of the audience. For her first song, she wears a black tie, tails and top hat similar to La Bessiere's: sexual ambiguity is conveyed by both dress and behavior. Sternberg is here using androgyny, characterized by cross-dressing, to convey campy incongruity through sexual masquerade. As Jack Babuscio states:

> To explain the relationship of Sternberg to camp it is necessary to return to the phenomenon of passing for straight. This strategy of survival in a hostile world has sensitized us to disguises, impersonation, the significance of surfaces, the need to project personality, the intensities of characters, etc. Sternberg's films—in particular the Dietrich films—are all camp insofar as they relate to those adjustment mechanisms of the gay sensibility.[20]

Babuscio's point is important in understanding Sternberg's attraction to sexual masquerade and disguise and in elaborating further on Sternberg's "ironic attitude toward his subject matter."[21] Irony, an essential element of camp sensibility that stresses stylization over content, contributes further to the notion of incongruity-as-camp. In Sontag's words:

> Camp is a vision of the world in terms of style—but a particular kind of style. It is a love of the exaggerated . . . of things being-what-they-are-not.[22]

Sexual masquerade (i.e., cross-dressing) here becomes a kind of Otherness. Its incongruity is somewhat different from the incongruity of the Otherness of the foreigner suggested by the first two scenes, but similar in its presentation through stylization of something-that-is-what-it-is-not.

Sternberg's history as a frequenter of the German cabaret scene may account for his fascination with cross-dressing,[23] since the German cabaret tradition was responsible for many nightclub acts that presented women as men or men as women.[24] In addition, Sternberg had seen Dietrich dressed in trousers at a social event, and was clearly intrigued with the prospect of dressing her in similar garb in his film.[25]

In a blatant expression of directorial arrogance, Sternberg demonstrates his desire to control even the erotic connection between

Amy in her androgynous cabaret costume (Jerry Ohlinger)

viewer and viewed (spectator and object) by concealing the well-known legs (the fetishized objects) from view, reshaping the erotic connection to produce a being, an Other, who appears to be what she is not.

Apparently, Sternberg's stubbornness served him well in a confrontation between himself and studio officials, who, upon seeing a brief trailer displaying Dietrich in formal male garb, rejected the idea as unrealistic (their wives wore "nothing but skirts") and impractical (a pair of trousers "could not be lifted"). But Sternberg stood his ground and got his way, later marveling immodestly at a creation that had actually influenced women to wear slacks.[26]

Adolph Zukor, Paramount's studio chief, spoke of how the trend had begun.

> Marlene's indifference to publicity was a major reason why millions of Americans today wear slacks. At one point our publicity department decided that new press photographs of Dietrich were needed. "I'm loafing around in slacks," she told Blake McVeigh, the publicity man assigned to get the pictures. "If you want to shoot me this way, all right" . . . she posed in her trousers and . . . the photographs were in great demand by the press. All over the country the stores were raided for their small supplies of women's slacks. The rage was on.[27]

Here is an example of how a star's extrafilmic life can reinforce her star presentation through promotion and publicity, extending the notion of incongruity (i.e., sexual ambiguity expressed through cross-dressing) beyond the limitations of the individual film.

In fact, Dietrich's appearances in slacks, both in her film roles and in her private life as well, began a real fashion trend for women in the thirties. Hollywood's time schedule for film releases and the unavoidable lag behind fashion worried studio executives. Their fear that the costumes worn in films would appear dated by the film's release date encouraged an attempt to make Hollywood, rather than Paris, the fashion trendsetter.[28] Relying on movies for advice about fashion, the public looked to studio designers as the fashion experts, and countless articles and photo layouts appeared in movie magazines such as *Photoplay* and *Screenland*, setting fashion standards more trusted than even those of *Vogue* or *Harper's Bazaar*.

Margaret Bailey sees the acceptance of slacks into public life as one of the major innovative fashion occurrences of the thirties, attributing the trend to Dietrich's star power:

> She was the first to wear slacks in public in 1931 in Hollywood, although everyone wore them on the studio lot. It is ironic that a woman renowned

for her femininity would launch a new vogue of fashionable masculinity.[29]

Rebecca Bell-Metereau attributes the fashion for slacks to sociological factors. The stock market crash allowed more women to enter the work force, and looking masculine was considered an asset.

Perhaps film directors and critics celebrated the masculine aspect of woman in an unconscious attempt to reconcile audiences to the economic realities of the day, when an increasing number of women were usurping the role of provider for the family.[30]

Dietrich's androgynous appeal, both in her private life and in her screen personae, was a quality seized upon by Sternberg, who frequently used sexual ambiguity teasingly, in an attempt to make ambiguous and incongruous the relationship between outward appearance and inner reality.

Cross-dressing can also be viewed as a political statement that utilizes costume to redefine the female self.[31] Simone de Beauvoir suggests that the definition of woman as female and man as human being forces woman into a position of male-imitation at those times when she most wants to be viewed as a human being.[32] And Susan Gubar suggests that the rise of "masculine" clothing as a pervasive political issue in the suffrage movement might support de Beauvoir's suggestion that women could actually seek a kind of self-definition by imitating men.[33]

Feminist film theorists Laura Mulvey and Claire Johnston view Dietrich's sexual masquerade as an indication of the absence of woman in male-dominated Hollywood cinema. Since woman is presented only in terms of what she represents for man, she becomes a manifestation of male narcissism, representing, through a process of displacement, the male phallus.[34] Further, the image of woman as sign within a sexist ideology is subject to the law of verisimilitude, the determinant of the impression of realism. Johnston blames this characteristic of Hollywood cinema for the repression of woman-as-woman and the celebration of her nonexistence.[35]

Johnston's argument is particularly interesting when applied to Sternberg's resistance to realism. Sternberg's style challenges accepted notions of reality by "breaking the illusion of realism,"[36] a strategy Johnston advocates as necessary for feminist filmmakers who seek to challenge audience assumptions and expose the falseness in traditional, capitalist representations of a so-called reality. His resistance makes Sternberg more of a revolutionary than he has here-

tofore been given credit for, and while his resistance has more to do
with an assertion of power than with a declaration of consciousness,
the result is a questioning of cinematic representation and its adherence to verisimilitude.

Sternberg's work also provides many examples of what Laura Mulvey interprets as fetishistic scopophilia in its transformation of the
represented figure (Dietrich) into a fetishized object, making it reas-
suring rather than, as a castration threat, potentially dangerous. Fetishistic scopophilia "builds up the physical beauty of the object,
transforming it into something satisfying in itself."[37] Mulvey claims
that

> Sternberg produces the ultimate fetish, taking it to the point where the
> powerful look of the male protagonist is broken in favor of the image in
> direct erotic rapport with the spectator . . . woman is . . . the direct
> recipient of the spectator's look.[38]

Mulvey further notes that there is no "mediation of the look
through the eyes of the male protagonist." She locates the film's most
highly emotional and dramatic moments as times when Dietrich is
alone. For Mulvey, the most important absence is that of the controlling gaze within the screen space.[39]

While it is true that Sternberg reveled in photographing Dietrich
alone, ejecting most crew members from the set during the long
close-up sessions and presenting her as a fetishized object in many
scenes, Mulvey has failed to mention important instances in which
the male protagonist does look directly at Dietrich. In both *Shanghai
Express* and *Blonde Venus,* for example, Dietrich is the object of the
male gaze, evidenced by close-ups and cutting, and is the source of
men's changes of heart. In *Morocco,* both Cooper and Menjou exercise fetishistic scopophilia—Cooper as a member of the audience at
Amy's performance and Menjou on board the ship in the opening
scene.

While feminist theorists such as Mulvey and Johnston provide an
essential challenge to traditional Hollywood cinema and its representational system, their analysis of Dietrich's masculine attire works
better as support of their theory rather than as a help in understanding Sternberg's schema. As Bill Nichols has suggested: "Clothing
weaves another strand in Sternberg's ideolect; it is another code contributing to the plurality of meaning. . . "[40] The analysis of one costume sign, i.e., Dietrich in male attire, isolates the sign from
Sternberg's schema. Costume, for Sternberg, is a major narrative/
thematic structural device in the complex textual system of his

oeuvre, and consequently requires an analysis that considers it as such.

Dietrich's appearance in top hat, tie and tails in the film's cabaret scene, besides its stylization of incongruity-as-camp, serves to extend the idea of sexual ambiguity beyond the mysterious figure of Amy Jolly. In this scene, Sternberg introduces the idea of the double by presenting Amy and La Bessiere dressed in the same formal attire.[41]

Sexual ambiguity is further highlighted by Amy's flirtation with a female member of the audience and its gestural repetition with Tom Brown. Amy removes a flower from behind the woman's ear, sniffs it, kisses the woman (a move partially concealed by Amy's top hat), and tosses it to Tom, who mirrors Amy's gestures by sniffing the flower and placing it behind his ear. In a later scene in Amy's apartment, Tom kisses Amy, a move concealed here by a fan, and Amy removes the flower from Tom's ear, tossing it away with a gesture that completes a complex circle of sexual crisscrossing.

While sexual ambiguity and reversal are recurring motifs in many of Sternberg's films (see, for example, *The Shanghai Gesture, I, Claudius* and *Jet Pilot* among the non-Dietrich cycle), their appearance in *Morocco* serves the film's thematic purpose. The reversal here is a sign of Sternberg's understanding of woman's position as both soldier and victim within a male-dominated society. Amy describes herself as a member of the Foreign Legion of Women and one who has come to Morocco to do as Legionnaire Brown has tried to do, i.e., to "ditch the past." But, as she explains, women "wear no uniforms—no flags—no medals when they are brave," so the struggle is one of constant self-definition. The expression of discomfort is not so much with the denial of woman's presence, as feminist theorists suggest, but with the lack of any satisfactory definition of woman either by society or by mainstream artists. Sternberg's vision of discomfort remains, as it does in so many of his films, more radical than sexist.

Cross-dressing can also be viewed as masquerade, an extension of an idea advanced by psychoanalyst Joan Riviere. Riviere believed that femininity or womanliness was a mask worn by women who needed to hide their essential masculinity so as to avoid personal anxiety and social pressure.[42] Primarily interested in the intellectual, professionally successful woman, Riviere suggests that for such a woman, the public display of intellectual proficiency signified an exhibition of herself in possession of the father's penis, thus resulting in guilt for having castrated him. Fearing horrible retribution for such a deed, the woman masqueraded as guiltless and innocent by "disguising herself" as a castrated woman, which often required some form of "feminine" behavior, such as a display of ineptitude concerning typically "male" skills or choosing typically feminine clothing.

Riviere's ideas were elaborated on by Jacques Lacan, who saw masquerade as the definition of femininity, since it was constructed as a referent to a male sign, i.e., feminine meant "not male." Lacan inverted Riviere's notion to postulate his own theory of femininity and masquerade:

> I am saying that it is in order to be the phallus, that is to say, the signifier of the desire of the Other, that a woman will reject an essential part of femininity, namely all her attributes, in the masquerade.[43]

It is Lacan's theory, elaborated on by the *Cahiers* critics, who saw the masquerade, virile display and inversion as erotic paradigms of *Morocco*,[44] that was generalized by Laura Mulvey in her work on visual pleasure in cinema.

Both the *Cahiers* critics and Mulvey, through their deductive analyses, fail to acknowledge Sternberg's utilization of costume-as-sign as an organizing principle, not only for individual films, but for his entire body of work as well. The fact is, Sternberg's attention to costume throughout his work displays a broader concern for masquerade, not always sexual, than is implied by either the *Cahiers* critics or feminist theorists.

Incongruity-as-camp continues in *Morocco* as a costume motif in the performance that directly follows the black-tie and tails number. In a brief dressing room scene, Amy is instructed by Lo Tinto, her boss, to sell her apples. The manager promises her ten percent of the profits. She is dressed in a black, brief outfit (one that closely resembles a modern one-piece bathing suit) and wears a serpentine feather boa around her neck. This costume is the inverse of the previous scene's male attire, and here her purpose is to "seduce" the men in the audience by masquerading as Eve the temptress. The costume also serves to further confuse the identification of Amy's sexuality.

After she sees Tom with Amy, the jealous Madame Caesar, wife of the officer in charge of Tom's regiment, provokes Arab men to attack him. Tom is arrested for fighting with them, and La Bessiere offers to use his friendship with Caesar to help free Tom. Following Tom's release, La Bessiere visits Amy in her dressing room (she is dressed again as the "apple-girl"), where he gives her an expensive, jeweled bracelet and asks her to marry him. She refuses his offer, weakly denying her love for Tom, who knocks on the dressing room door to say goodbye. Following La Bessiere's gracious exit ("I think you two want

Amy "selling her apples" to Tom (Gary Cooper). (Jerry Ohlinger)

to be alone"), Tom asks Amy to accompany him to Europe on his de-
sertion. Amy leaves to perform her cabaret act, assuring Tom of her
return. While she is out, Tom explores her dressing room, finally notic-
ing the bracelet given Amy by La Bessiere. Whistling admiringly, he
tries on Amy's top hat, looks at himself in the mirror, replaces the hat
with his kepi, and writes a message on the mirror: "I changed my mind.
Good luck!" Here, costume gesture and sexual crossover suggest the
rigidity of the double standard as seen from Tom's position. He cannot, as he looks into the mirror, see things from her perspective, and he
becomes another of Sternberg's morally rigorous men. Like Herbert
Marshall in *Blonde Venus* and Clive Brook in *Shanghai Express,* he im-
poses his own restrictions on sexual freedom. La Bessiere, less morally
rigorous because of his own worldliness, is more understanding of
Amy, and their similar costumes reflect his empathy. While Tom and
Amy are both sexually ambiguous characters, there is clearly a limit to
the crossover, a double standard Sternberg exposes through costume
that serves as a kind of gesture. Amy does not fit the categories of other

women with whom Tom is more familiar—the veiled Moroccans, the native prostitutes, and the promiscuous Madame Caesar (also veiled at one point). He is clearly uncomfortable with her difference. Later, Amy will become more "recognizable" as she joins the rear guard of women who follow their men into the desert; but Sternberg's discomfort with that choice will be made clear through an analysis of the shooting of the last scene.

Tom's hat exchange also signifies an inability to see himself as a civilian. His final choice in favor of his own kepi indicates his preference for continuation in the world of the professional soldier, a world in which he has discovered his self-definition.

Amy and La Bessiere (Adolph Menjou) as analogues. (Jerry Ohlinger)

The costume similarity between Amy and La Bessiere continues throughout the film. When Tom leaves, both Amy and La Bessiere are dressed in black tuxedos. Both are again dressed in black at their engagement dinner, he in a tuxedo, she in a black evening dress and a pearl necklace. When she learns of the return of Tom's troop, she cannot keep herself from rushing out to find him, and she catches her necklace on a chair, breaking the string of pearls. The event suggests a loss of control and a breaking of her agreement with La

Bessiere. When she returns to the dinner party to say that she will try to find the wounded Brown, La Bessiere offers to go with her. His explanation to his guests ("You see . . . I love her. I'd do anything to make her happy") and their similar costumes in the next scene (they both wear white, belted overcoats) makes it clear that La Bessiere is in the same position with regard to Amy that Amy is in with regard to Tom. Both are willing to sacrifice themselves for the person they love. In fact, La Bessiere is a member of Amy's "rear guard" just as Amy, in the film's last scene, becomes a member of Tom's.

The film's last scene, referred to as "one of the most absurd of all time,"[45] combines earlier elements of incongruity-as-camp with costume gesture to summarize the film's major thematic concerns. As Amy waves goodbye to Tom (she is dressed here in white chiffon), she suddenly makes a decision. After a wordless goodbye to La Bessiere, she walks toward the desert, following the troops and joining the rear guard of women. With a typically significant costume gesture, she removes her scarf from around her neck, and places it around her shoulders, giving the accessory the more gypsy-like look of the women of the rear guard. She then follows Tom into the desert, discarding her high-heeled shoes in a final gesture of renouncing prior values. The scene involves incongruity-as-camp through its presentation of absurdity (Dietrich in the desert, cultural clash) and exaggeration through costume gesture. Throughout the film, costume has been used to signify crossover, interchange and concealment, a strategy Sternberg used in other films (*Blonde Venus* in particular) to signify the search for a proper place, and the suitability or unsuitability of various roles. In *Morocco*, all of the main characters seek self-definition through costume or costume gesture, but it is only Tom who is unable to change. While La Bessiere has changed from being "the most exacting bachelor in the world" to becoming a member of Amy's "rear guard," and Amy has become one of the camp followers, Tom has remained the soldier. His uniform, worn throughout the film, conveys his intransigence.

In his presentation of incongruity (Dietrich walking into the desert in high heels), Sternberg has undercut the apparent romanticism of Amy's sacrifice with disturbing filmic images, and we are left with an ending that conveys the director's uneasiness about Amy's choice and the traditional Hollywood ending,[46] a discomfort explored in greater detail through his attention to costume in *Blonde Venus*.

In fact, camp, as a reflection of Sternberg's ironic attitude toward his subject, is merely one of many means used by the director to transform content through stylization. Throughout his career, Sternberg positioned himself at a distance from his material, permitting many variations on the theme of ironic attitude, several of which are evident in *The Devil Is A Woman.*

The Devil Is A Woman, the last of the Sternberg/Dietrich collaborations, is, in many ways, Sternberg's most personal film. It recapitulates concerns expressed in earlier films, as well as reflects his complex relationships with Dietrich as star, as character/persona, and as woman.

The film also marked the end of Sternberg's association with a team that had afforded him the kind of control he required to exercise his artistic will. With the dissolution of the Sternberg/Banton/Paramount/Dietrich collaboration, the director would never again be as attentive to the costume signs that resulted from the union of director, designer, studio and star. In this last major union of the collaboration, Sternberg even took credit for the photography, listing Lucien Ballard as his assistant.

The critical and financial failure of *The Scarlet Empress,* which did not even return its $900,000 budget, as well as changes in Paramount's executive hierarchy, caused a serious weakening of the Sternberg-Dietrich alliance. Ernst Lubitsch replaced B. P. Schulberg as Paramount's head of production, immediately exercising his authority by insisting on a title change for Sternberg's film from *Caprice Espagnol* to *The Devil Is A Woman.*[47] While the alteration angered Sternberg (he suggested that "altering the sex of the devil was meant to aid in selling the picture, although it did not do so")[48] Lubitsch's choice of titles actually seems more appropriate to the film's content and Sternberg's concerns. It suggests the cumulative fears of both artist and man in a waning professional and personal relationship.

In his announcement that this would be their last film together, Sternberg expressed his apprehension about any continuing association.

> Miss Dietrich and I have progressed as far as possible together. My being with her any further will not help her or me. If we continued we could get into a pattern which would be harmful to both of us.[49]

The declaration sounds suspiciously like the misgivings of one who recognized a dangerous relationship. In fact, the statement might easily have been made by either of the two leading men in *The Devil Is A Woman.*

The autobiographical nature of the film is evident in the physical resemblance between Sternberg and his leading male, as it was in

Morocco. Andrew Sarris indicates that Sternberg never before "seemed as visible as he does here in the saturnine silhouette of Lionel Atwill,"[50] while John Baxter refers to Atwill as "an exact replica [of the director], even [down] to [the] moustache and impeccable clothing."[51] John Kobal furthers the connection by suggesting that Sternberg is "Pasqualito, the dreamer who falls in love with the romantic illusion and is consumed and destroyed by it."[52] Kobal quotes Fritz Lang as saying, "Von Sternberg created a person and then that person destroyed the creator."[53] Sternberg himself saw the film as a "final tribute to the lady [he] had seen lean against the wings of a Berlin stage in 1929."[54]

But even given his decision to end the association with Dietrich, Sternberg could not have anticipated the film's ensuing difficulties. The Spanish government lodged an official objection to the film, provoked, according to Sternberg, by its depiction of incompetence among the civil guard, which seemed unable to control rioting revelers at a carnival.[55] Herman Weinberg cites the presentation of a civil guard officer (Atwill) made ridiculous by a "loose woman" as the reason for Spain's objection.[56] In either case, the Spanish Minister of War threatened to ban all Paramount films in Spain unless the print was withdrawn from circulation. It appears that the fear of such a restriction, coupled with the precariousness of a proposed commercial treaty between the United States and Spain, caused Paramount to capitulate.[57] The film was shown only at the Museum of Modern Art, and remained out of circulation until 1959, when it was sent to the Venice film festival. It returned to limited circulation in 1961.[58] In any case, it was not only the Spanish government that objected to *The Devil Is A Woman*. Referred to by Sternberg as his "most unpopular film,"[59] it received negative reviews and poor box office results.

The Devil Is A Woman was based on a sadomasochistic novel by Pierre Louÿs entitled *Woman and Puppet*. The title comes from a painting by Goya *(Tapices XLII)* in which four women toss a male puppet around in a blanket.[60] Sternberg credits John Dos Passos with helping to write the screenplay. In the story, an older man named Pasqual (Lionel Atwill) warns a younger man (Cesar Romero) about having a destructive liaison with the spectacularly beautiful and dangerous Concha Perez (Dietrich). Antonio (Romero), having been smitten earlier by the seductive Concha, agrees never to approach the woman again, but her allure makes it impossible for him to keep his word. When Pasqual, who has also expressed his commitment never to see Concha again, finds the younger lovers together, the former friends become active rivals, and a duel is scheduled to settle the issue. Pasqual, clearly the better marksman, does not even take aim and is shot by Antonio. The latter is arrested, but later freed as a result of Concha's promises to the chief of police (Edward Everett Horton). Concha and Antonio prepare to leave the country together, but Concha changes her mind, presumably to return to the wounded Pasqual.

Sternberg's mise-en-scène is cluttered with the familiar nets, veils and confetti of earlier films, but here the decor seems even more firmly woven into the film's narrative fabric than has been previously the case. As Andrew Sarris suggests, Sternberg's decor is not mere background, but rather the subject itself,[61] supporting the idea of mise-en-scène as mystery, and of mystery as cinematic essence. And while the campy style of *The Devil Is A Woman* does not approach the baroque design of *The Scarlet Empress* in its excess, it remains a film in which "nature was not permitted to intrude on Sternberg's grand design."[62] On the contrary, in *The Devil Is A Woman*, Sternberg returns to methods explored in earlier films, with a particular emphasis on the use of costume, masks, nets, cages, and screens and metaphors of disguise and masquerade.

The film begins with a frenzied carnival, reminiscent of both the gangsters' ball in *Underworld* and the masquerade in *Dishonored*. Police chief Don Paquito (Horton) identifies the carnival as a time when "every crook will try to take advantage of the masquerade." Frames cluttered with confetti, balloons and masked revelers convey Sternberg's interest in obscuring the apparently accessible image, while oversized and contorted mask-heads recall the grotesque gargoyles of *The Scarlet Empress*. The first close-up focuses on Antonio Galvan, who uses the disguise of a reveler to hide his true identity as a political offender with a price on his head. Antonio employs his slingshot to burst the balloons that obscure the first sight of Concha in her carriage. But an unobstructed view of Concha is not yet possible, since a view of her face, even in long, languorous close-up, is still obscured by pom-poms which, attached to her veil, surround her face like tiny satellites. Throughout the film, Concha wears veils that create an air of enigma and inaccessibility about her character. One never knows when Concha is telling the truth, and her face, half-hidden by her costume and the decor, maintains this ambiguity. As suggested by Andrew Sarris, the motif of the masks is carried through all of Concha's "maddening deceptions,"[63] and applies as well to Antonio and Pasqual, the latter attempting to conceal desire beneath his mask of "intelligence and urbanity."[64]

Confetti and crowds become the elements of mise-en-scène that prevent Antonio from reaching Concha once he has seen her, and

Concha Perez (Dietrich) glimpsed through her pom-poms and veil in *The Devil Is a Woman*. (Jerry Ohlinger)

his entanglement by the decor foreshadows the later entrapment of his soul as her lover. Cages of several sorts—bird cages and jail-like gates that lead to Concha's and Pasqual's respective homes—serve as signs of entrapment throughout the narrative.

While nets, veils and cages maintain mystery and signify deception, the major costume metaphors in *The Devil Is A Woman* center once again around Dietrich. As in *Dishonored* and *Shanghai Express*, Sternberg is interested in the costume metaphor of disguise, introduced here in the milieu of the masquerade. But in *The Devil Is A Woman*, disguise has deadly overtones, and the title, while not Sternberg's first choice, provides an appropriately provocative metaphor in its implication of the fatal woman. In addition, the extraordinarily ornate costumes and a variation on the theme of disguise affords Sternberg the opportunity to explore ideas regarding glamour, ideas centered around his star and her costumes. Here, more than in any of his previous efforts, Sternberg relies on elements of design as distancing devices to signal inaccessibility, mystery and danger. Such design elements as exoticism, evidenced by the foreign and unfamiliar Spanish costumes, and elaborateness (they are clearly Banton's most complex designs) serve to complicate the costume's look and stress concealment. The sharp, diagonal lines and stiff fabrics visually emphasize the theme of hardness that accompanies the image of the fatal woman.

The fatal woman is not, of course, an idea that originated with Sternberg. The femme fatale has existed in literature since Eve and Salome, and in art since the Sphinx, while the tradition in cinema dates from the silent film era of Theda Bara and D. W. Griffith. But whatever the medium, the similarities among femmes fatales are eternal. According to art historian Patrick Beale,

> No matter where the artists and authors found their subjects, these women all bear a marked family resemblance to one another. They are pale, proud, mysterious, idol-like, full of perverse desires yet cold at heart. The link between eroticism and death is always present, as is an atmosphere of perverse cruelty. . . . For many artists, it hardly mattered whether they painted Helen of Troy, Judith or Morgan-Le-Fay. The subject was always perceived in the same terms: malignant, threatening, destructive and fascinating.[65]

The classic femme fatale as described above strongly resembles Dietrich's characterization of Concha, but Sternberg's creation goes a step further in transforming his fatal woman from an object of lust to an object of vilification and she bears a striking resemblance to the sadomasochistic ideals of Baudelaire and Swinburne.

[Baudelaire's] poetry expresses an ambivalent attitude toward women, compounded of reverence, desire, fear and contempt. . . . It was necessary for Baudelaire to view the object of his desire as evil and monstrous. On a drawing he made of his mistress, Jeanne Duval, the "black Venus" of his poetry, he wrote the motto "Quaerens quem devoret" ("seeking whom she may devour"). . . . Baudelaire's behavior demonstrates how reverence can turn to fear, and fear to hatred . . . and masochism.[66]

Swinburne's description of "cruel, imperious" women and the men who long for death at their feet are even more closely associated with masochism than his admired French contemporary's. In fact, Swinburne's poem, *The Flogging Block,* celebrates the pleasures of flagellation, and sadomasochistic relationships between men and women figure prominently in Swinburne's other writings.[67]

Resembling Sternberg's creation even more closely, however, is the femme fatale epitomized by Prosper Mérimée's Carmen. Based on a gypsy the author had met in Spain, Carmen became the prototype for many working-class women and prostitutes in nineteenth- and twentieth-century literature. She also provided the central character for Bizet's opera. Like Bizet's Carmen, Sternberg's Concha works in a factory and is constantly visited by men who recognize her as the most beautiful woman there. Henri Agel remarks on the comparison with the Merimee/Bizet creation, commenting also on costume.

The Vamp, incarnated here by Concha Perez, a species of super-Carmen, hideous as a result of so much cruel and metallic splendor, evoked those devouring females of the Italian screen as in d'Annunzio's deliriums. She appears at the end all in black, adorned with sinister magnificence, shortly before which she has sung a ballad the very German sadism of which blends well with the atmosphere of a decadent Spain, just as Cocteau might have dreamed it.[68]

John Kobal elaborates on Agel's comparison between Sternberg and Cocteau, alluding to the latter's vision of the artist's own death "'masquerading as a woman'" in *Orphée.*[69]

The idea of Concha as the fatal woman finds its most complete fulfillment in the sadomasochistic relationship between the woman and her self-destructive lover, Don Pasqual. Again and again, Pasqual leaves and returns to Concha, alternating between self-restraint and submission. In his uncontrollable lust for Concha, Pasqual has lost not only his dignity but his honor as well, having been forced to resign his commission as a result of their scandalous affair. For Sternberg, the loss of the uniform means the loss of honor, and Pasqual is clearly a man who can no longer be trusted. In lying to himself, he also lies to Antonio: having promised never to see Concha again, he is hardly capable of keeping his word.

The last scene, an ambiguous presentation of Concha's refusal to leave the country with Antonio and her insistence on returning to the wounded Pasqual, reflects the dichotomy of the femme fatale: is she returning to save her lover, or does her black-clad figure serve to ensure his death? Andrew Sarris prefers the latter interpretation, extending its reference to Sternberg's personal and professional autobiography:

> Black quite simply means death, and Marlene may be one of many deaths for both Atwill and Sternberg, the death of art, of poise, of poetry, of inspiration, of the will to continue.[70]

Concha's dual nature is also visible in costume signs that often suggest beauty can be concealed beneath a veneer of innocence. In her first meeting with Don Pasqual, she appears, seated in a train, dressed in a nun-like habit and wearing a large, prominent crucifix. Annoyed by a dancer who continually jostles her, Concha trips the dancer, exposing the savagery beneath this facade of innocence. Following the melee, the habit-like covering falls away from her face, revealing the earring and exaggerated makeup of the enchantress. Cecelia Ager refers to the way in which both Dietrich's stylized makeup and costumes as well as Sternberg's photography signify eroticism.[71] In fact, it seems clear that the hard lines accentuated in her face by the exaggerated makeup were further emphasized with lighting that highlighted its angularity, giving her, along with "gaudy jewelry" and "flashy costumes,"[72] a much harsher appearance than she had in any prior film.

The bizarre costume designs by Travis Banton combined Spanish traditional couture and the high fashion look of thirties couture.[73] Her clothes were specifically designed to harden her image with inventive variations of singularly seductive visuals and countless diagonal lines.[74]

Throughout the film, the stiff combs Concha wears in her hair, as well as the inflexible fans she carries, add to the impression of callousness. The message is that this woman cannot be emotionally moved or manipulated, and her resistance is indicated by the rigidity of her look. Her insensitivity is further conveyed by the way in which light bounces off of the sequined fabrics and glittering combs she wears throughout the film. At one point, Sternberg suggests her hard-heartedness with a necklace of black hearts. She wears this necklace when she persuades Pasqual to buy off her contract, and then immediately abandons him for a matador who waits outside.

Concha's duality expressed in her nun-like costume. (Museum of Modern Art Film Stills Archive)

The hardness motif continues throughout the film, changing only at the end with Concha's last costume. When she leaves Antonio, deciding to return to the wounded Pasqual, she wears a costume of much softer lines than any she has worn previously in the film. In fact, the chiffon dress and sloping hat with veil of matching fabric more closely resemble contemporary high fashion than do the other, more exotic, Spanish-influenced clothes used throughout. Here, the humanity of her decision is commented on by the director, who identifies with the older man who is his analogue. In having Concha refer to her unglamorous past ("I used to work in a cigarette factory"), Sternberg reminds us of all that Pasqual did for her, a self-serving reference to his own relationship with Dietrich. Concha's return to Pasqual is, pari passu, a wish-fulfillment for the director.

The extent to which Sternberg actually designed the costumes for *The Devil Is A Woman* is difficult to determine. Dietrich took credit for some of the ideas, acknowledging Sternberg's authority over conception and approval.[75]

Concha's "hardness" expressed in the sharp edges of her costume. (Jerry Ohlinger)

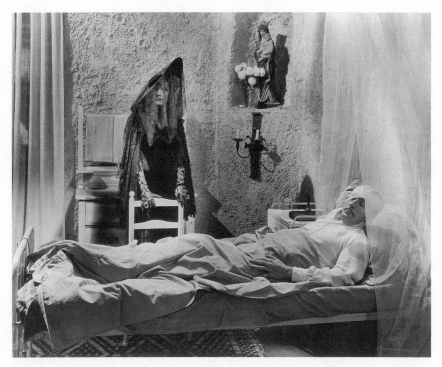

Concha in softer lines as she visits Pasqual (Lionel Atwill) on his deathbed. (Museum of Modern Art Film Stills Archive)

David Chierichetti attributes the ideas for the exaggerated, almost comic costumes to Sternberg, while suggesting that the "bulk of the creative work was nonetheless Banton's."[76] Vreeland and McConathy report that Banton employed textures and amassed details (e.g., spangles, sequins, stockings with elaborate clocking) at Sternberg's urging, echoing "detail with detail, the lace of a mantilla caught in the lace of a parasol that was amplified by the lace through which the camera saw the scene."[77] The multiple layers of fabric and trim created an elaborateness of detail which further obscured an image already partially concealed by other elements of mise-en-scène.

Due in part to the costumes, Dietrich is more glamorous in *The Devil Is A Woman* than ever before, even if some of the effects border on the comic. But Sternberg was clearly serious about glamorizing his star in their last professional joint effort, and glamour for the director meant far more than mere sartorial festooning. In fact, Sternberg's concept of glamour—a concept that undoubtedly affected his approach to Dietrich in all of their films together, but which finds its most complete fulfillment in *The Devil Is A Woman*—

is an idea that deserves serious attention, since it plays an important role in Sternberg's resistance strategy.

For Sternberg, glamour meant enchantment, and more specifically, meant being "provocative, tantalizing, entrancing, fascinating, ravishing and bewitching."[78]

Especially interesting about Sternberg's definition of glamour is his attention to the provocative nature of the image and its association with the photographer's vision. Clearly Sternberg viewed the filmed photographic image as an artist's medium, much like a painter's palette or a sculptor's stone—an unformed material, subject to the artistic will and manipulative creativity of the director.[79] And while Sternberg had respect for Dietrich's potential, he clearly saw her as another color on his palette, always under the control of the craftsman.[80] In more specific language, Sternberg described his primary tools as light and the play of other elements of mise-en-scène, which create an air of mystery and inaccessibility.[81]

Through his use of hard lines, stiff fabrics and the manipulation of light as it bounced off of textures, Sternberg found a way to literalize theories of glamour, locating them in the elaborate costumes of The Devil Is A Woman. In addition, Sternberg's insistence that glamour cannot be achieved by a mere recording of reality further supports the director's emphasis on the exercise of artistic will in the achievement of his goals.

But even more appropriate to The Devil Is A Woman than the above declarations is Sternberg's association of glamour, defined as an imposition of artistic will on a representation of reality, with the legend of the beautiful woman, specifically, the femme fatale.[82]

In giving credit to Dietrich's "formidable personality," Sternberg may have provided a clue about why his attempts to express the essential nature of the medium found their most complete fulfillment in the Dietrich cycle. For it was Dietrich who provided Sternberg with a central focus for his artistic struggle. And while she may have been a "formidable personality," she was, as a woman-to-be-looked-at, subject to the manipulation of the director, who created a fraudulent image and presented it in a highly manipulated form that bore little resemblance to reality.[83]

Herman Weinberg attributes Sternberg's "glamorous" style to Paramount's acknowledgment of public taste:

> For Morocco, Sternberg abandoned the realistic style of The Blue Angel for the "glamorous style" of Hollywood. Marlene had been signed by Paramount to a long-term contract. She had to be groomed to the American taste and the American taste called for glamour—not realism.[84]

Concha in one of her many glamorous costumes. (Museum of Modern Art Film Stills Archive)

Glamour, for Sternberg, describes a complex artistic strategy for controlling the "realistic" tendencies of cinema through the tools available to the director—tools such as camera and composition. In addition, glamour focuses on woman, specifically on Dietrich, making her the object of decoration through both photography and, more appropriately, through the compositional element of costume. In the same way that light and other elements of mise-en-scène decorate Sternberg's image, often taking the form of excessive visual clutter or exaggerated decor, costume decorates the image of Dietrich, often taking the form of stylization and excess.

The Devil Is A Woman marks both the end of the Dietrich cycle and the conclusion of Sternberg's use of costume as a central metaphor in his films. In ending his association with his star, Sternberg relinquished his main object of display and surrendered to studio domination. John Baxter reports that Sternberg felt "liquidated by Lubitsch," Paramount's new production manager, and the director became increasingly aware that his eccentricities would no longer be tolerated. Following the premiere of *The Devil Is A Woman*, Sternberg's contract with Paramount was terminated.[85]

After *The Devil Is A Woman*, Sternberg seemed to lose some of his artistic spunk. Without the freedom he had been given at Paramount, particularly by Schulberg, without Dietrich, without Banton and without Paramount's commitment to European style as support for his vision, Sternberg's artistic will could not remain as strong as it had been. In an interview in 1961, he spoke of his own decline following the Dietrich cycle.

> I stopped making films in 1935. . . . My ideas about the cinema became more precise in the light of my experiences. I was tired of seeing studio opposition to any creative ideas of the cineaste at the different stages of its expression. Whereas a painter uses his brushes, canvas and colors, following only the bent of his imagination, the film director has to consider other men and human material. After a trip around the world, I wanted to work according to certain principles; for instance, that we should be concerned to create expressive effects achieved in literature—and I hoped to work with more freedom. A lot of unhappy events prevented me from this, such as the tragic events of those [later years].[86]

His most artistically productive period over, Sternberg continued to make films that used costume signs to explore the nature of cinema, but with his loss of control, he would never again approach the richness of the cycle of films made in collaboration with Paramount, Banton and Dietrich.

6

Sternberg vs. History: *The Scarlet Empress* and *I, Claudius*

The Scarlet Empress (1934) represents Sternberg's first venture into period, permitting the director's imagination to compete with history, and presenting Sternberg with an opportunity to exercise his artistic will against a backdrop of historical reality by using devices of stylization and excess.

The film's titles first announce that the story is based on history—specifically, on the diaries of Catherine the Great of Russia. But Sternberg challenges history almost immediately: the next title cards suggest vagueness and fairy tale rather than historical truth.

About two centuries ago, in a corner of the kingdom of Prussia, lived a little princess—chosen by destiny to become the greatest monarch of her time—Tsarina of all the Russias—the ill-famed Messalina of the North.[1]

Like *Blonde Venus*, therefore, *The Scarlet Empress* begins with a suggestion of fairy tale that prevents us from taking the film too seriously as an "authentic" historical reconstruction.[2] But more importantly, the idea of fairy tale serves as a variation on Sternberg's typical artistic resistance to both his medium and his material. In *The Scarlet Empress*, reality is represented by historical content but not by the way that content is expressed; imagination is exercised in the form of stylization and excess, emerging most notably in costumes and decor.

While the tension between reality (as represented by history) and imagination (as represented by fairy tale) is introduced immediately and concerns the film's larger visual scheme, it is, perhaps, most useful for the purpose of this study to consider the way in which history and period are usually conveyed in film, and how Sternberg has adhered to or deviated from more traditional approaches.

The "realistic" medium of film presents some problems for both designer and viewer. Historical films, supported by a viewer's usual willing suspension of disbelief, are supposed to take place in "realistic" settings, whereas historical theater can take place in merely suggested or stylized locations. The assumption is that the settings and costumes of historical films must necessarily be as lifelike as possible. According to clothing historian Anne Hollander, however, period costumes in film are in fact as distorted as many stage trappings, since the camera's scrutiny and the eye of the viewer must be satisfied by acceptable, contemporary details of beauty and fashion, even though such details might be historically inaccurate.[3] Designer Walter Plunkett has emphasized the importance of tempering period details with an acceptable contemporary veneer:

> I think you took the period thing and knocked off an awful lot of things that truly dated it and then blended in a little of what the modern eye would accept as smart. Of course in doing any biography of an actual person, you took what they had worn or were painted in as a basis because it had to look like that. Then maybe soften the things that to the contemporary eye looked ludicrous about a period and substitute a blend of modern.[4]

Travis Banton, like most designers of the thirties, had an interest in keeping costumes fashionable. Because of the time lag, often a year or two, between a film's conception and its final release date, Hollywood designers were always concerned about the stylishness of their designs. One way to insure that film costumes would maintain their currency was to use advance studio publicity to present a film's costumes as fashion trendsetters. In a typical interview with Banton designed to publicize the film as well as to ignite the interest of fashion-conscious women, the designer sounds more like a couturier:

> The new Dietrich costumes in *Catherine the Great*, in which she is incredibly beautiful, will emphasize more than ever the importance of shoulders and bust. Her gowns are brought way down in the front to the lowest possible degree showing the deep line between the breasts. The back is also very low. Women in the audience, seeing how exquisitely beautiful and feminine she looks, cannot help being influenced in their own clothes.[5]

In fact, in order to protect their design investments, film costume designers emphasized Hollywood's greater influence over American fashion than that of Paris. In an article entitled "Hollywood Snubs Paris," William Gaines suggests the possibility of Banton's influence on fashion:

Some of his most fascinating creations are worn by Marlene Dietrich in *The Scarlet Empress*. This is a costume picture, to be sure, but there is always the possibility of some detail of dress or coiffure, when exhibited by such a favorite as Dietrich in such a picture, starting a widespread fad. Who can say yet?[6]

In one respect, the modification of period costume to meet contemporary fashion standards is a form of stylization, and while not of the same type as that produced by excess, it is an approach that modifies the truth of history through artistic interpretation and commercial awareness. A similar approach was to be utilized throughout *The Scarlet Empress* as Sternberg directed his designers to alter history to his liking. Banton himself said of his approach to period:

Miss Dietrich's costumes in that picture represented perhaps the finest and most beautiful collection of clothes I've ever had the pleasure of designing. They were expressive of the period's fashions without being mere stereotyped copies of sketches found in books. Rather, I placed myself mentally in the position of a designer of the middle eighteenth century.[7]

The sets, exaggerated to the level of the baroque, were the work of Hans Dreier, Paramount's art director for thirty years. In 1923, he had come to Hollywood from the German UFA Studios, where he had undoubtedly learned a great deal about exaggeration, stylization and distortion in an artistic climate of expressionism. Dreier's excessive style was perfectly suited to Sternberg's passion for alteration and exaggeration, and the two worked together from 1927 to 1935. John Baxter describes the results of Dreier's opulent sense of design on the look of Paramount films as "gilded, luminous (and) rich and brocaded as Renaissance tapestry." His backgrounds were seldom used, as they were in Metro films, as mere background, but rather play a role "guiding, and occasionally dictating, the feel of a film."[8]

Dreier's inventiveness became a trademark for the look of Paramount films of the thirties, and descriptions of his style indicate a vision sharpened by excess.

Although he could turn out sets in the standard Hollywood style, he was a truly inventive designer who added to them a fantasy, a mysterious, disquieting atmosphere rare among American designers of the period. . . . The designs for Sternberg's *The Scarlet Empress* (1934) are also reminiscent of the baroque. This is a strange world not far removed from surrealism, peopled with Byzantine statues and paintings, which one enters through enormous doorways and takes by assault, riding upstairs on horseback.[9]

While it seems clear, both through their long association and similar design viewpoints, that Sternberg and Dreier shared a general outlook that resulted in exaggeration, it was still Sternberg who dictated the look of the film. Though he chose to have the sets decorated by the Swiss sculptor Peter Balbusch and the German painter Richard Kollorsz, themselves visual stylists, Sternberg took complete credit for the film's visual presentation.[10]

In attempting to explain his artistic approach, Sternberg, referring to his efforts as his "peculiar tendency to prove that film might well be an art medium,"[11] attempted to justify his alteration of history, identifying his stylization as "a re-creation, and not a replica" of Catherine's Russia.[12]

Advance publicity for the film revealed the film's stylization and departure from historical truth with the apparent hope of justifying Sternberg's liberties with period. *The Daily News* reported in November 1933 (using the film's original title, later changed by studio executives):

> When screen audiences see *Catherine the Great* . . . they will see a Russia that never existed, but an infinitely interesting and colorful Russia brought to life by a staff of skilled workers, designers, artisans, sculptors and painters. Von Sternberg and his art director, Hans Dreier, decided to abandon historical accuracy and give the story of Catherine a stylized Russian background, designed to build up the drama of the story.[13]

But such prior justification for stylization did not deter the uniformly vitriolic reviews at the time of the film's release. Sternberg was unanimously condemned for subordinating plot and characterization to an overpowering visual style that bore little resemblance to history.

Richard Watts, Jr., writing for the *New York Herald Tribune*, suggested that the film probably set new records for "sheer idiotic affectation."[14] *New York Times* reviewer André Sennwald called the film "a bizarre and fantastic historical carnival," attacking Sternberg's departure from history as "a succession of overelaborated scenes, dramatized emotional moods and gaudily plotted visual excitements."[15]

Time magazine's review suggested that Sternberg's "tedious hyperbole" suffered by comparison to director Paul Czinner's British film, released several months before *The Scarlet Empress*.[16] Supervised by Alexander Korda and starring Elisabeth Bergner and Douglas Fairbanks, *Catherine the Great* was praised for its fidelity to history while given leeway for its excesses. André Sennwald wrote that "it clings considerably closer to history than do most kindred pictorial subjects,"[17] and Richard Watts, Jr. called it "a handsome, lavish, dramatically impressive and beautifully acted drama of striking skill and power" even though "highly sentimentalized and far from an accurate picture of the amorous German princess."[18]

But Watts's apology for the film's departure from history had more to do with the playing down of Catherine's love affairs than it did with stylistic excess, since the Czinner version made only passing, and then rather vague reference, to the empress' sexual liaisons.

In effect, the contrast to the earlier film's adherence to history exposed Sternberg's heavy-handed ways to a critical audience that had not been offended previously by the director's perversity. Suddenly, Sternberg was in the unfortunate position of having literalized his artistic tensions in a historical milieu. In *The Scarlet Empress*, Sternberg's artistic will takes a stand against history, a history made more accessible by the release of the earlier film. In fact, beginning with *The Scarlet Empress*, Sternberg's critical reception was to become increasingly problematic, and his subsequent film efforts were greeted with skepticism. What was once considered an acceptable style now became categorized as sheer hyperbole and distortion.

But while his excess was another exercise of his artistic resistance, Sternberg was not completely ignorant nor unconcerned about the importance of signaling period through costume details. He understood that movie stars must first be made to look attractive and, second, to look historically correct. Surface truth in visual detail had to be meticulous because of the camera's intense scrutiny. Expensive fur needed to be expensive fur. Armor needed to be armor and not a theatrical substitute, which from a distance can look enough like armor to fool the viewer. Such surface truth can serve as a signal of period that satisfies an audience's need for historical realism. As Anne Hollander suggests, greater efforts to be accurate are unnecessary; costume signals, not details, can be used to convey period, and details are free to be historically incorrect.[19]

It seems clear that both Banton and Sternberg, each perhaps for somewhat different reasons, must have understood the need for flexibility with historical details regarding both costume and setting. While the costumes in *The Scarlet Empress* are accurate in terms of general period—that is, the eighteenth century—they are inaccurate in terms of the specific portion of the century in which events actually occurred. The style of clothing worn by the men and women in the film dates from a period between 1750 and 1780, a period characterized in women's dress by paniers, a rather awkward, hoop-like underskirt of whalebone held together by ribbons and covered with a taffeta or brocade fabric. While paniers were introduced in France in 1730, the panier style of the costumes in *The Scarlet Empress* did not appear until later in the century. About 1750, the hoop was divided into two sections, called pocket paniers, in which the paniers were formed by pulling draped fabric through pocket holes in the skirt.[20] The film opens at a time when young Catherine (here still called Sophia) appears to be a child of eight or nine. Since Catherine was born in 1729, the actual date should be somewhere around 1737 or 1738. Both her mother's costume, which contains pocket paniers, and her father's costume (a coat whose front slopes away from the waist and whose sides, pulled back and unflared, but buttoned or tacked so that they form a tucked tail at the back) are styles that were not introduced until after 1750 even in France (the fashion center for most courts around Europe). Sophia's father also wears a cadogan wig, a style using rolls along sides rather than curls, and not introduced until 1755. It seems clear, then, that Sternberg and Banton chose a later period of the eighteenth century for their costume signals, rather than the more accurate Watteau style, which would have been correct for the first half of the century. Actually, the Watteau style, more fluid in its lines than the paniers, would have been almost too conservative against the later, outrageous decor of the Russian court, while the more awkward styles of the latter half of the eighteenth century serve to complement the stylized settings.

Even with stylization an apparent consideration, however, the presentation of the star and contemporary standards of beauty and style are still carefully regarded. Early in the film Dietrich's hair, unlike the hairstyle of the other women in the film, is not arranged in the eighteenth-century Madame Pompadour style, but rather in an acceptably contemporary shoulder-length style with side curls and bangs that flatter and frame Dietrich's angular face. As William Gaines suggested in his *Photoplay* article on Hollywood film and fashion, Banton's hairstyle for Dietrich was likely to be imitated by "every little high school girl in the country."[21]

In contrast to the other women of the court, she wears costumes of chiffon and other diaphanous fabrics that do not gibe with the historical accounts of the wide use of brocades and other heavy fabrics. Dietrich's accessories are also often historically and geographically incorrect, as it is unlikely that feathers appeared in the frigid Russian climate as frequently as they did as trim for Dietrich's costumes.

It seems clear that Dreier, Banton and Sternberg, after satisfying

Sophia (Dietrich), recently arrived at the Russian court (from *The Scarlet Empress*). (Photofest)

contemporary audience taste and maintaining star beauty, proceeded to exaggerate and stylize the costumes to the level of the baroque, sacrificing history to a chosen visual style. As reported in the London *Times* in May 1934, when *The Scarlet Empress* was released in England,

> The subject of the film is not Catherine nor a particular episode in history, but the Russia of the past seen in a fantastically distorting mirror, extravagantly Oriental, infinitely sinister, holy and horrible. Almost every effect is got by scenery and settings. Human beings are continually mixed with statuary which seems far more alive than they and the violence of decadent Byzantine art, often still further degraded to a kind of German expressionism, is beyond anything which the most powerful actor can achieve. . . . The ferocious icons, the statues of martyred saints, the ominous and weighty architecture do all the work and carry the whole burden of the story.[22]

Sternberg answered his critics with typical indignation, defending his excesses with reminders of his concern for budgetary propriety and artistic parsimony.[23]

In fact, Sternberg took great pride in exposing the errors of those who charged him with extravagance, among them, studio production chief, Ernst Lubitsch. He pointed out that he had tried to economize by reusing a crowd scene from *The Patriot*, an earlier Lubitsch film, and reveled in the fact that Lubitsch had not recognized his own work. He was keenly aware of the irony of Lubitsch's complaints about the film's excesses.[24]

While his defensiveness may seem like more pompous ranting, it is clear that period reviewers, influenced by the earlier, more historically faithful version of Catherine the Great's story, had had their realist sensibilities jolted by Sternberg's baroque interpretation of history, and, in their outrage, had failed to acknowledge artistic license. More recent critics, such as Tom Flinn, have recognized the uniqueness of Sternberg's approach to history, crediting the director with a personal vision that bordered on the artistically courageous. He contrasts Sternberg's approach to the facsimile approach used by Griffith in *The Birth of A Nation* both to justify his depiction of scenes that might offend audiences with their racism and to impress viewers with the young medium's ability to visually recreate history. Flinn presents Sternberg's approach as an alternative to Hollywood convention as well as a defiance of the medium's capacity to record literal events.[25] Once again, we can observe the multilevel complexity of Sternberg's perversity, as he continued to challenge the ontology of the photographic image[26] through stylization and excess.

In addition to Flinn's praise, Sternberg received plaudits from other critics impressed with his imaginative vision of history. Herman Weinberg reports that Henri Langlois, curator of the Cinémathèque Francaise, after having seen *The Scarlet Empress* in 1964, cabled Sternberg with the following message praising its similarity to and apparent influence on Eisenstein:

Have just seen marvelous *Scarlet Empress*. Stop. What grand film. Stop. All *Ivan Grozhny* comes from your film. Stop. All my respect and admiration.[27]

G. W. Pabst, the German director who had become associated with "street realism" (a style of filmmaking notable for its concern with social realities, but heavily influenced by Eisenstein's theories of montage) also expressed his admiration for the visual charisma of Sternberg's version of history:

I look at the screen. . . . I don't believe what I am seeing, but there it is! I think I am losing my mind, it is so incredible![28]

Andrew Sarris goes further in praising Sternberg's shattering of "the decorum which was spreading over the American cinema like a shroud."[29] He suggests that Sternberg's excess, in contrast to the earlier and far less interesting Czinner version, served to highlight Hollywood's visual conservatism and Sternberg's artistic pluck.[30]

Sarris attributes the stylization and exoticism of Sternberg's last two Dietrich films (*The Scarlet Empress* and *The Devil Is A Woman*) to a need to hide from the censors. He suggests that Sternberg retreated into an exaggerated period in order to conceal threatening sexual innuendo.[31] Sarris' point is important in contributing to an understanding of Sternberg's motivation to explore period, but the implications of the director's decision to delve into history are more far-reaching than a need to escape censorship. In fact, the move into the past provides Sternberg with another arena in which to exercise his artistic will. Its posing as a reminder of the past highlights the peculiarities of the director's own personal vision, emphasizing his directorial presence.

Leo Braudy suggests that Sternberg's stylization creates a power struggle between his characters and the costume and decor that constantly appear to stifle them. According to Braudy, Catherine the character struggles against the exaggerations of Sternberg the director, attempting to maintain her own discrete identity in a world of overpowering decor that threatens to envelop her.[32]

In contrasting Sternberg's treatment of history with that of Rossellini in *The Rise of Louis XIV,* Braudy notes the difference between
Sternberg's myth and "elaborate baroque fantasy" and Rossellini's
historical documentation. Sternberg's control of the film's visual
world (an analogue of Catherine's control of her own physicality
through control of decor) is contrasted with Rossellini's stand-
offishness as a director.[33]

While history provided Sternberg with a general arena of realism
in which to exercise his imagination and artistic will, both costume
and decor became his methods of resistance. Individual costumes
often signified specific struggles within the general tension between
history and imagination.

In *The Scarlet Empress,* Catherine's maturation from a little German princess to a powerful Russian empress is impeded by forces
signified by the frequently oppressive costume and decor.

In the introductory section, in which the child Sophia is still played
by Dietrich's daughter, Maria Siebert, the attending doctor (who is
also the public executioner) declares that the child's health will im-
prove if she wears a harness for a year or two. The reference is the
first of many to the idea of costume as entrapment. In the very
next scene, the adolescent Sophia is introduced (now played by an
energetic, breathless, hyperactive Dietrich) and the costume, decor
and performance suggest a freedom and innocence that will soon
be subjected to the will of others and the requirements of political
expedience. Sophia wears a white chiffon dress layered with ruffles—
perhaps the most physically unrestrictive of all her costumes—and
plays on a swing that moves back and forth towards the camera. The
erotically teasing motion permits the lens to look up her skirt, though
the view is ultimately obscured by her pantaloons. Sternberg suggests
here that the apparent natural freedom of this princess is actually
controlled by others as she leaves her playground (the most open,
natural space in the film) only to learn of her arranged marriage to
Peter of Russia. A title card presents the conflict between free will
and destiny, as well as again emphasizing history:

> On March 15, 1744, Princess Sophia Frederica departed for Russia, full
> of innocent dreams for the future, and completely unaware of the fate
> which was to transform her into the most famous woman of her day.[34]

As a furtherance of the visual-sexual tease which introduces Dietrich as Sophia (the shot of her swinging toward the camera, revealing
her pantaloons), Sternberg repeats the revealing, erotic gesture in an
element of decor. On the night when Peter and Catherine are to

marry, Sternberg uses a clock figure to recall the earlier erotic gesture and announce its darker implications here. As Robin Wood has suggested, Sternberg uses the striking of ornamental clocks to announce important moments in "the personal and private violation that accompanies the rise to power."[35] Wood refers specifically to a figure of a woman, opening her dress to reveal nudity, but fails to make a connection between this revealing erotic gesture by an element of decor and the earlier gesture. The suggestion is that Catherine, her sexuality now completely under the control of others, has been reduced to the level of a mechanical puppet, a mere doll which has to perform at the appointed hour of her wedding night to provide Russia with a male heir to the throne.

Wood does, however, make an interesting connection between the shot of Sophia on the swing and an earlier shot which dissolves into it. While the young Sophia is told grotesque tales about the horrors of Russia's power-mad monarchs (a foreshadowing of her own fate), we are shown visualizations, perhaps even fantasies, of the stories. Most of the images have "sado-erotic overtones,"[36] and the last one, which dissolves into Dietrich on the swing, is that of an almost naked man who has become a human bell clapper, dangling helplessly upside down inside the bell. The dissolve remains on screen for a few seconds as a superimposition so that bell clapper and girl become one image. The apparent contrast between the freedom of movement of Sophia on the swing and the helplessness of the man in the bell is qualified by the use of the dissolve as a filmic device implying either comparison *or* contrast. Perhaps, Wood suggests, the implication is that the girl's freedom is merely illusory, and her inability to control her fate is expressed in the metaphor of the man's helplessness.[37]

Wood's interpretation supports the notion of the struggle between Catherine's will and her own destiny, a struggle which continues as a costume/decor motif throughout the film. Her struggle against fate presents a potential answer to the question of why Banton and Sternberg may have altered the historical period of the film's costumes. In fact, the more historically accurate Watteau style, with its significantly less rigid, more free-flowing lines, would not have conveyed Catherine's struggle as effectively.

As Wood further suggests, the dissolve from the bell to the bell-shaped skirt furthers the connection between images of entrapment and costume signs.[38] At one point later in the film, Catherine is strapped into the cage-like paniers, and restrictive costume imagery continues throughout her rise to power. Costume is usually cumbersome, tight and generally repressive. In fact, if period itself is a fashion restriction specifically defined by lines and shapes, rules and

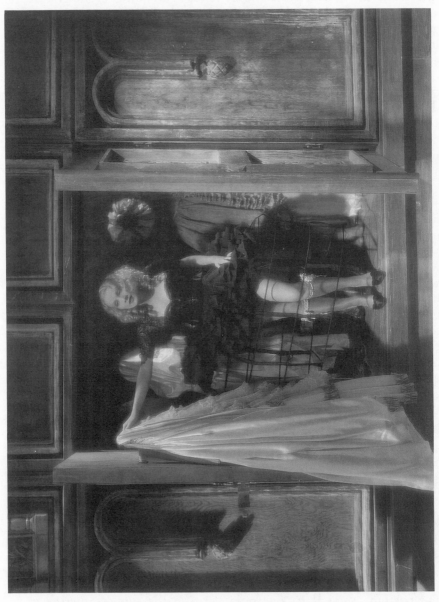

Catherine (Dietrich) in the cage-like paniers that signify her entrapment. (Photofest)

regulations, then in a larger sense Catherine is restricted by fashion and period.

The multilevel attention to the struggles between freedom and entrapment through costume and decor reflects the growing frustrations faced by an artist who was beginning to lose favor with critics and general public alike. Even in his use of Dietrich, Sternberg's struggle to display control takes the form of grotesque distortion. The sexual appeal that was once so teasingly seductive now reaches the level of the fatal in both *The Scarlet Empress* and *The Devil Is A Woman*. In both these films, Sternberg seems obsessed with a need to control his creation with costume characterization that borders on caricature. As Joyce Rheuben has suggested, even those moments of emotion that appeared in earlier films seem presented in the last two Dietrich vehicles as "perversity, parody or even burlesque," making Sternberg's humor "very dark indeed."[39]

In fact, Sternberg's artistic will goes beyond the darkly humorous, almost to the point of desperation, in *The Scarlet Empress*. He struggles to maintain control in a medium whose "license" for such control is closely linked to critical and public acceptance. Robin Wood suggests that Catherine's struggle to control her own destiny can be interpreted as an analogue of Sternberg's own artistic struggles, both with Hollywood and with the public.[40] Sternberg's struggle for artistic freedom and control continues to be exercised in more aspects of the mise-en-scène than merely costume. The wedding scene between Peter and Catherine, for example, combines oppressive elements of mise-en-scène (clutter, statuary, tight framing) with actors' gestures and costume signs, all of which work together to convey the sense of entrapment, desperation, and loss of free will experienced by the previously hyperactive and uninhibited young Sophia. In fact, the transformation from innocent princess to mature, powerful, cynical empress is a metamorphosis introduced in a title card and later reflected in costume signs:

> . . . her ideas of romance outraged—her name altered, her religion changed and pushed like a brood mare into the preparation for her marriage to a royal half-wit.[41]

In the scene that precedes the wedding scene, the princess Sophia is fitted with new clothes and her hairstyle is changed, a procedure over which she has no control, since it is supervised by the empress. The scene is important in continuing the idea that her freedom will be threatened by entrapment and her free will controlled by destiny.

The wedding scene that follows represents the summit of Catherine's oppression in the film.

The scene uses tight framing and a cluttered mise-en-scène; the frame is filled with grotesque statues and is dissected by diagonal lines of staircases and hangings that sectionalize the image into tiny, confining compartments. Combined with Catherine's desperate looks and the cutting from Alexei (her lover) to Peter (her crazed bridegroom) and back to Catherine again, the image emphasizes her entrapment and apparent destiny. In the close-up of Catherine's face, Sternberg obscures the image by shooting through a gauzy veil, but he does not obscure her desperation, here characterized by the flickering candle, nearly extinguished several times by her impassioned breathing. It is a scene saved from a permanent sense of despair only by the following scene, which suggests that Catherine has not yet surrendered to the apparent inevitability of her destiny. Following the wedding scene, Catherine recovers some of her earlier exuberance. Having just finished her daily ride, she rushes breathlessly up a flight of steps and is stopped by Count Alexei, who angrily questions why she has become inaccessible to him. The reference to horses and riding, and the rush up a flight of stairs foreshadow her triumphant ride and breathless coup in the film's last scene, and suggest here her unwillingness to surrender control over her destiny. She wears a black riding outfit, with feathers trimming a tricorn hat. This is an early modified version of her final hussar's uniform, with its more traditionally masculine lines. In fact, Catherine's movement to autonomy, which progresses significantly after the scene in which she learns of Alexei's infidelity with the empress, is reflected in her costume. Even the use of her handkerchief as sartorial prop signifies greater control in both the political as well as the sexual arenas, and she symbolically castrates her half-witted husband by draping it over his threateningly outstretched sword.

Catherine's move toward the accession to power and the control of her own destiny is signified, most importantly, by the "Russianization" and formalization of costume. Her garments are made from heavier fabrics (taffeta and velvet) than the earlier chiffons and organdies, and her dresses are trimmed no longer with feathers, but with the more "Russian" fur. According to David Chierichetti, the choice of fur was less a matter of aesthetics than economics and politics, since Banton had been directed by Paramount head Adolph Zukor, a former furrier, to use as much fur as possible in the hope that the fur trade would be boosted by its presence in the film.[42] Banton himself suggested that the use of fur was part of his attempt to maintain authenticity:

1495-141

Catherine becomes more "Russianized" in her dress. (Museum of Modern Art Film Stills Archive)

In several scenes, like the wedding ceremony in the cathedral, I strove
for somewhat barbaric effects with sables, furs, jeweled headdresses,
black and gold combinations—but the average spectator, of course,
missed many authentic details over which I had worked days and weeks.
They just added to the general glitter.[43]

Banton's statement sounds like the cry of a man whose meticulous
design work had been swallowed up by the overpowering, baroque
visuals of the film, and there is evidence to indicate that certain of
the costume details were authentic. One particular gown was fashioned from a fabric of rose-point lace purchased from a Russian
woman. The precious fabric had been originally made in a small
town in Russia by people who presented it to the last Czarina, and
Banton was taken with both its beauty and its history.[44] But the
iconography of costume in Sternberg's films is far more important
than authenticity, and while the tension between period and stylization creates an interesting battleground for Sternberg's artistic struggles, there is something in the history of the period itself which may
explain Sternberg's attraction to it. In his biography of Catherine the
Great, Henri Troyat refers to the "deceptive facade" of Russian court
life.

> Day by day she [Catherine] was discovering the true Russia—barbarous,
> cruel and wretched behind an appearance of civilization. Everything here
> was merely a deceptive facade. The efforts of Peter the Great to Europe-
> anize his country had brought about only superficial changes. Since the
> ukases of "the Builder" the Russians shaved their heads, tricked them-
> selves out in wigs, dressed in the French fashion, took snuff and danced
> as in Vienna or at Versailles. Yet these men and women who claimed to
> be "progressive" were completely ignorant of real Western culture. . . .
> Here the ladies-in-waiting vied with each other for the most elegant ward-
> robes, but most of them did not know how to read. They were exclu-
> sively preoccupied with intrigues, dancing and fashion.[45]

The actuality of Russian court life, filled with deceptive appearances, provides a remarkably appropriate setting for a director so
personally resistant to appearances, and ironically authenticates
Sternberg's choices. For while some of the costumes may have been
historically accurate, most were not; authenticity was constantly sac-
rificed to stylization throughout the film.

The appearance vs. reality theme is furthered in Catherine's most
dramatic transformation and maturation, which occurs after she is
sexually betrayed by Count Alexei and begins to concentrate on
converting sexual efforts to political power struggles. After dis-

covering Alexei's infidelity with the empress she breaks her emotional tie with him by tossing his miniature portrait out of a window. In attempting to retrieve it later, Catherine becomes involved with another soldier, the first of many sexual liaisons which are to continue throughout the film. She gives birth to a son, clearly not her husband's child, and in an interesting shot, Sternberg shoots her behind gauzy netting to obscure the reality of the image and emphasize that things are not as they seem, as the rejoicing multitudes outside the palace acknowledge the birth of an heir to the throne. From this moment on, Catherine's transformation is purposeful and directed; she uses her sexuality as a means to gain the support of an army whose power she requires. As the title card proclaims:

> Firmly entrenched in her position by now being the mother of a future Tsar, Catherine discarded her youthful ideals and turned to the ambitious pursuit of power.[46]

Sternberg reflects her transformation in the Russianization and hardening of her costume and demeanor, and in the next scene, she is coifed for the first time in the harder lines of the Pompadour hairstyle (although other women in the film wear this hairstyle, most notably, the abrasively "un-Russian" empress and Peter's companion, Countess Elizabeth). The Russianization is most evident in the scene in which Catherine reviews the troops, adding more and more soldiers to her list of lovers and supporters. In fact, the uniform here suggests a likeness or sameness among her potential lovers. It emphasizes their interchangeability, and Sternberg drives the point further home in a later scene in which Alexei, the now-rejected lover, meets Orloff, his replacement, in the same passageway in which Catherine suffered her own rude awakening about Alexei's infidelity. The men resemble each other both in features and in dress, enough to be almost mirror images.[47] Catherine no longer cares who her lover is, but only how he can satisfy her sexual ambitions and needs. In this scene, she wears a black costume whose bodice resembles a uniform, with military fastenings across the chest and a Russian fur hat and muff. Costumes such as this one alternate with more feminine, antihistorical, suggestive and strapless off-the-shoulder gowns with see-through chiffon skirts, further emphasizing the growing connection between sex and power. Finally, sexual and political power merge within the single, glitteringly white hussar's costume of the film's last scene.

As he did in both *Morocco* and *Blonde Venus*, Sternberg turns to cross-dressing as a signifier of shifting power, sexual ambiguity, anal-

Catherine in pompadour hairstyle. (Jerry Ohlinger)

ogy and ultimate crossover into the less restrictive, more liberated world of androgyny. And here, as in *Blonde Venus*, the androgynous costumes signify the end of a journey to self-discovery. It is important, however, to distinguish between the cross-dressing of *Blonde Venus* and *Morocco* and that of *The Scarlet Empress*. Whereas in the two earlier films the Dietrich character was a performer, such is not the case in *The Scarlet Empress*. The emphasis, therefore, is less on intrafilmic performance and display and more on character transformation and metamorphosis through a "Russianization" and masculinization that reflect the critical blend of sex and power that help Catherine attain her position. Dressed in a gleaming white hussar's uniform, Catherine's image is contrasted with earlier images of the weak, womanly Peter. The ecstatic ride up the palace steps and the fiendishly breathless pose with her horse in the film's last shots are, according to Joyce Rheuben, Sternberg's suggestion of Catherine's supposed sodomitic propensities.[48]

But most important about this final scene, in addition to Stern-

Catherine in her hussar's costume, about to ride up the palace steps. (Jerry Ohlinger)

berg's typical connection, through costume, of power with sex, is the ride itself and its statement regarding the artist and his medium. Thundering through the decor that has previously engulfed and over-powered her, Catherine rides past immobile statues which can only gape helplessly at her. Here, in a remarkable turnabout, Sternberg has literalized his own artistic struggles with Hollywood commercial cinema by shifting control from decor to character. For if, as Robin Wood has suggested, Catherine's survival in "a world into which she was plunged" represents Sternberg's struggle to survive in the commercial cinema of Hollywood,[49] then Catherine's triumphant ride to power represents Sternberg's fantasy of the triumph of imagi-nation and artistic will over both history and the medium in which he worked.

Following his unsuccessful term at Columbia, and while re-covering in a hospital from an intestinal illness, Sternberg was ap-proached by producer/director Alexander Korda to film Robert Graves's *I, Claudius*. Based on earlier, apparently painful, efforts working with Charles Laughton, Korda had decided not to direct the film himself.[50] In addition, Dietrich had agreed to waive Korda's $100,000 debt to her (still outstanding from a film they had made together entitled *Knight Without Armor*), if he could find a project for Sternberg to work on.[51] Laughton, long an admirer of Sternberg's work, tried, on several visits to the hospital, to persuade the director to accept the project, plying him with gifts of grapes and undiluted praise.[52] As a result of Korda's offer and Laughton's importunity, Sternberg accepted the assignment.

There were enormous difficulties with Laughton, who could not find his character and who required more coddling than Sternberg was capable of giving him. In addition, a serious automobile accident hospitalized its star, Merle Oberon, with a concussion and facial abrasions. As a result, the project was shelved. Several of those in-volved with the production, as well as Korda's son, Michael, saw the accident as a godsend, a "deus ex machina" that had "saved the day." Switching to another leading lady was impossible since so much foot-age had been shot, and the accident thus provided a reason for col-lecting insurance. This fortuitous circumstance saved Korda from the financial bankruptcy of an apparently inevitable commercial failure.[53]

Some of the footage retained from six weeks of shooting was com-piled and edited together with interviews of the project's partici-pants: Oberon, Robert Graves, Emlyn Williams (who played Caligula), Flora Robson (the empress dowager), a script girl who had worked with Korda for many years, the film's costume designer

Sternberg, Merle Oberon and Charles Laughton on the set of the unfinished *I, Claudius*. (Museum of Modern Art Film Stills Archive)

John Armstrong, and Sternberg himself. It was made into a BBC documentary entitled *The Epic That Never Was*, and the seventy-five minute film provides some insight into a project which appears to have returned Sternberg, however momentarily, to the position of complete control that was so crucial to his art. As reported in the trade press during preparations for the shooting of the film:

> Josef von Sternberg has taken over his Denham offices and is busy with preparations for *I, Claudius*. . . . He personally supervises all suggestions from set designers, costume experts and property departments, as well as working on final touches of the script.[54]

In fact, Sternberg himself said he "designed the costumes."[55] John Armstrong, credited as designer, explained that the director had insisted on certain details of costume which conflicted with the historical accuracy that his own research had uncovered. For instance, Sternberg wanted sixty vestal virgins, not the six prescribed by Roman ritual, because it "looked impressive."[56] He insisted on their wearing bras and panties under transparent veils, though Armstrong remarked on the unlikelihood of their being so accoutred, "since they were sworn to chastity." The costume designer summed it up by saying "it looked lovely, but it had nothing to do with the Roman religion."[57]

As a designer who was under contract to Korda, Armstrong had worked on earlier Korda efforts, among them the previously mentioned Czinner production of *Catherine the Great* (1933), the film against which Sternberg's version of history, *The Scarlet Empress*, was harshly measured by critics of the period. It seems ironic that Sternberg would ultimately find himself working with a team that had earlier provided an antithesis to his own approach to history. In fact, based on Armstrong's testimony, Sternberg's self-credit for the costumes, and the insistence on elaborate, expensive sets, *I, Claudius* might well have emerged as another example of a work in which Sternberg could have displayed his antihistorical spirit against the backdrop of history. What remains, based on testimony and extant footage, is merely an impression of what might have been.

The City as Cinema: *The Shanghai Gesture* and *Macao*

Both *The Shanghai Gesture* (1941) and *Macao* (1952) are examples of Sternberg works which shift their focus of concern from star to city.

Of the films which followed the Dietrich cycle, *The Shanghai Gesture* is the only one (besides Sternberg's last film, *The Saga of Anatahan*) over which the director was able to exercise the kind of control he had been used to earlier in his career. In particular, its concern for exoticism, as well as its interest in deception, disguise, and racial and sexual ambiguity make *The Shanghai Gesture* a typically Sternbergian work.

In 1941, the British producer, Arnold Pressburger, approached Sternberg with an offer to film the controversial John Colton stage play. This had been attempted by others on several occasions to no avail, due to the rigors of Hays Office censorship. But Sternberg and his collaborators (Jules Furthman, Karl Vollmoller, and Geza Herczeg) changed the setting from Mother Goddam's brothel to Mother Gin Sling's casino, making veiled references to the original that satisfied the censors while remaining faithful to the spirit of the Colton version. Herman Weinberg reported that "Sternberg was back in his milieu again," working with complete directorial freedom and a sympathetic producer who gave him "absolute authority over every department, including the casting."[1] John Baxter referred to the film as "the last classic Sternberg film," controlled in its decor and concept and typical in its atmosphere of earlier Sternberg efforts.[2] Sternberg himself explained his interest in the project as an interest in giving assistance to a friend (Pressburger) who needed help in securing "a foothold in a land in which he was a stranger." At the same time he took credit for the launching of Victor Mature and Gene Tierney as "stellar attractions."[3] But Sternberg's own coldness about the film may have had more to do with critical response than lack of interest. The film was not well-received; it was referred to by

Bosley Crowther of the *New York Times* as "so utterly and lavishly pretentious, so persistently opaque and so very badly acted in every leading role but one that its single redeeming feature is that it finally becomes laughable."[4] The story concerns the degradation of a young woman named Poppy (Gene Tierney), whose father, the supposedly honorable Sir Guy Charteris (Walter Huston), is assigned to clean up the corrupt city of Shanghai. He begins with the closing of its most notorious night spot, the casino owned by the tough-minded Mother Gin Sling (Ona Munson). Poppy becomes involved with the slimy Dr. Omar, Doctor of Nothing (Victor Mature), and her moral decay through drink, gambling and sex is swift and ultimately fatal. At a strange gathering celebrating the Chinese New Year, a time when people "pay their debts," it is revealed that Mother Gin Sling is actually Poppy's mother. The news devastates the entire family (mother, father and daughter), and in an act of perversion, the mother kills the disobedient daughter, while the father fatalistically accepts this act as his punishment for prior sins.

The film is difficult to summarize, since so much of its effect lies in its visual atmosphere, set in yet another typically exotic locale. The main problem, however, is that without the persona of Dietrich to act as a vehicle for his artistic concerns, Sternberg must create a substitute for the missing woman. Unable to find a suitable human replacement for Dietrich, Sternberg turns to the city as the embodiment of enigma and ambiguity once symbolized by his star. In the first title card description of the exotic locale, Sternberg hints at its complexity:

> Years ago a speck was torn away from the mystery of China and became Shanghai. A distorted mirror of problems that beset the world today. It grew into a refuge for people who wished to live between the lines and laws of customs—a modern tower of Babel. Neither Chinese, European, British nor American, it maintained itself for years in the ever-increasing whirlpools of war. Its destiny, at present, is in the lap of the gods—as is the destiny of all cities. Our city has nothing to do with the present.[5]

Sternberg's use of the city as a mysterious, exotic place of perversity and deception becomes the metaphor for cinema as well: a seductively strange locale attractively beckoning yet ultimately elusive.

Frank Krutnik refers to Shanghai's metaphorical significance as "a model of the exotic, the known and alluringly strange."[6] In his analysis of the exotic as melodrama in *The Shanghai Gesture*, Krutnik uses the term exoticism to describe Sternberg's visual style.

> Exoticism is a term frequently used in describing Sternberg's style: e.g.,

what is seen as his animation of the "deadspace" of the image, a hyper-charging of the visual field by set and dress design; stylized object and character emplacement; the use of veiling, masking and lighting effects; and the measured dissolves and the slow, exploratory camera tracks and cranes.[7]

In fact, Krutnik's description of the exotic visuals further supports the link between the seductiveness of the city and the allure of Dietrich. Both were presented as fascinating objects of the look:

The "film"—taken to mean the operation of the non-scriptual processes—operates, however, by creating and exploring the "exoticism." The visuals are made extremely seductive in the tension between the Oriental murals and the formal Western dinner suits, e.g., the increasingly grotesque but fascinating appearance of Mother; the geometrical attraction of the seemingly endless circles of the Casino; and the stylized groupings of the actors and the many extras. Visually, the film offers itself as a beautiful, pleasurable object to be looked at and loved.[8]

In his substitution of the city of Shanghai for the missing Dietrich, Sternberg has compensated for the loss of his star by replacing her with another appropriate vehicle for the continuation of his exploration of cinema.

In addition to the larger metaphor of exoticism around which the film's visuals are organized, Sternberg uses clothing metaphors to represent inaccessibility. Character ambiguity, a distancing device used in several earlier films (particularly *Dishonored* and *Shanghai Express*), becomes a means to further investigate the realm of the exotic through deception, disguise, androgyny and miscegenation. Not only is it the city that eludes racial labeling (see opening title card description above), but its inhabitants are equally ambiguous. Dr. Omar refers to himself as a "thoroughbred mongrel, related to all the earth . . . born under a full moon [of a] mother who was half French and part of the Dark Ages [with a] father who was Armenian." Poppy turns out to be the Eurasian daughter of Mother Gin Sling and Sir Guy; the bartender, who sounds Russian, claims he has no country; and European characters speak to Asians in pidgin English which the Asians clearly recognize as patronization. Early in the film, Poppy's escort comments on the racial mixture among the casino's patrons ("Half the faces are Eurasian"), while Poppy herself expresses an attraction to the mystery of racial ambiguity.

It smells so incredibly evil . . . it has a ghastly familiarity, like a half-remembered dream . . . anything could happen at any moment. . . .

Look at that Arabian [Omar], or whatever he is. I wonder . . . does he
sleep in his fez? What do you think he is?

Character/actor relationship adds to the ambiguity. Mother Gin
Sling is played by Ona Munson, a Caucasian heavily made up to
look Chinese; her American accent contrasts starkly with her bizarre
Asian costumes. A rickshaw driver who speaks Russian with an
American accent is played by Mike Mazurki, "too big to be Chinese," as Sir Guy observes, yet doing the menial work which would
not be done by a Westerner. Montgomery How, the shady Oriental
whose dealings include drug-and jewelry-smuggling, speaks perfect
English, but often, when convenient, affects noncomprehension.
Since minor Asian characters are played by Asians, it seems clear
that an East/West opposition is being created by racial differences
between actors and the characters they portray, an opposition that
works to reinforce notions of ambiguity and mystery.

In addition, characters are, as they were in *Shanghai Express*, disguised or hiding a secret. Poppy introduces herself as Miss Smith,
and only later is her true identity (which has remained a secret even
to her) fully revealed. Sir Guy Charteris is revealed to be the Victor
Dawson who married the innocent Chinese girl (now Mother Gin
Sling, whose hard exterior disguises her own vulnerable past) and
fathered the child she thought was dead. Other characters are in debt
to the casino, or have purchased black market jewelry for illicit love
affairs. In general, the characters wear numerous kinds of masks
(some literal, some figurative), a favorite Sternberg costume sign
often used to maintain inaccessibility.

Louis Audibert refers to the masks as a metaphor for deception
and mystery.

The faces of *The Shanghai Gesture* are progressively revealed to be
masks, the truth of which must be sought for beyond them, in the enig-
matically glittering eyes. . . . Their names are themselves deceptive: Gin
Sling, mistress of pleasure and gambling, of the painted face, the long,
drawn-in eyelashes, the white forehead crowned by a cunning coiffure,
strange and artificial; Sir Guy Charteris, of the European mask, the
enterprising smile, the ignoble past. His daughter (Gene Tierney), with
the turned up nose of an insolent, greedy child, whose features come
apart, hairdo tumbles down, cheeks swell up.[9]

The metaphor of the mask, visible in Mother Gin Sling's heavy
makeup, as well as in the obvious makeup of faces transformed from
Western to Eastern, is also present in Sternberg's use of the Chinese
New Year celebration as masquerade. Once again, as in *Dishonored*

and *The Devil Is A Woman,* Sternberg returns to the carnival to explore questions of revelation and concealment. The Chinese New Year celebration taking place outside the casino, cluttered with masked revelers and costumed merrymakers, serves to obscure the image and stress concealment. The composition of the masquerade's frames is simulated in the pull-back dollies and tracks-forward that reveal the dizzying movement of Mother Gin Sling's casino. Marcel Oms comments on the film's decor and its communication of mystery,[10] while John Baxter writes of the film's visual exoticism, referring specifically to the way in which decor and costume express oppositions between movement and stasis, oppositions Sternberg has explored in *The Salvation Hunters* and *The Scarlet Empress.*[11]

The exotic as impediment to transparency is carried throughout the film's visual design in Oleg Cassini's costumes, a curious blend of the chic and the bizarre, which effectively depict the film's East/West dichotomy. Mother Gin Sling, often resembling a carved ivory goddess, with hard, sharp lines accentuated by heavy fabric and sculptured hairdo, wears "extra-Oriental" clothing, a stylized version of the Oriental look that seems almost grotesque in its exaggeration. But the stylization appropriately reflects the distance between the Eastern mother and the Western father (Sir Guy's clothes are characteristically British-conservative). The gap is bridged by the daughter, who combines the sinful amorality of both parents, and pays with her death for both her own degradation and for their sins.

Androgyny is another source of Sternbergian ambiguity. Dr. Omar, "the poet of Shanghai and Gomorrah"—the pleasure-seeker whose slithery sensuality conceals the nothingness of his false title—is one of several sexually ambiguous characters. As O. O. Green (Raymond Durgnat) has suggested,

> Impotence and sodomy are the film's half-concealed motifs. The white men—Eric Blore with his crutch (a Tennessee Williams-type crutch), Albert Basserman with his wry half-confession of impotence, the third card player, who seems to prefer boys, are hardly less masculine than Omar, the fatal man.[12]

Omar has become Sternberg's replacement for the femme fatale. He is a fatal androgyne[13] whose cool indifference ensnares the naive but passionate Poppy.

The gesture used by Omar to conceal a kiss—a gesture characterized by Andrew Sarris as "ridiculously furtive," since it is shot from "the far side so that Mature is framing rather than concealing the kiss as far as the movie audience is concerned"[14]—concisely summarizes

Mother Gin Sling (Ona Munson) in one of her bizarre costumes from *The Shanghai Gesture*. (Photofest)

The androgynous Dr. Omar (Victor Mature). (Photofest)

several of the film's major concerns. Omar's attempt at concealment is, rather, a revelation in its exposure of both the kiss itself and, as Sarris points out, "the ridiculousness of the Tierney-Mature relationship."[15]

But more importantly, the gesture, a curious blend of concealment and revelation because of the angle from which Sternberg shoots it, serves as a metaphor for the duality of both the city and the cinema, capsulizing Sternberg's ongoing concerns with the mysteries of his medium.

Macao (1952) was the second of Sternberg's films for Howard Hughes, and while the director appears to have had even less control over this assignment than he had over the ill-fated *Jet Pilot*, the film still shows evidence of Sternberg's visual style as well as of his continuing interest in costume signs.

Sternberg explained his agreement with Hughes as part of a bargain which he hoped would lead to further work and more autonomy.[16] Expressing regret over having accepted the assignment, Sternberg complained about his lack of control and the diffusion of authority over decision making.[17]

In addition to its numerous overseers during production, the film, in typically idiosyncratic Hughes style, was not released until eighteen months after shooting had been completed, and several scenes were reshot by Nicholas Ray. While Herman Weinberg says the only recognizable evidence of Sternberg is some "telling atmospheric shots,"[18] there are several interesting reminders of earlier works. The film's treatment of exoticism, for example, is reminiscent of *Shanghai Express, The Devil Is A Woman, The Shanghai Gesture,* and Sternberg's next and last film, *The Saga of Anatahan.* Its use of the woman as a performer recalls *The Blue Angel, Morocco, Blonde Venus,* and *The Devil Is A Woman.* Its reliance on the costume metaphor of disguise recalls *Shanghai Express* and *Dishonored.*

The film relates the story of the chance encounter between two drifters, one a singer named Julie Benson (Jane Russell), the other a fugitive named Nick Cochran (Robert Mitchum), who is unable to return home to New York because of a "little hassle over a redhead" during which he shot a man. The two meet on board a ship that also carries Lawrence Trumble (William Bendix), a detective disguised as a dealer in trinkets. His assignment is to lure a cabaret owner and jewelry smuggler named Halloran (Brad Dexter) beyond the three-mile limit so that he can be arrested by international police. Cochran gets mixed up in Trumble's plans. He ultimately avenges Trumble's death by turning in Halloran, and leaves Macao with the sultry singer for the island-like isolation of which they have dreamt.

In *Macao,* Sternberg once again turns toward Eastern exoticism, and here, as with *The Shanghai Gesture,* it is the city that provides Sternberg with an opportunity to explore cinema. Without Dietrich as the object of enigma and the perfect model for the clothes which shroud the female body in mystery, Sternberg focuses his attention on locale, making Macao a surrogate for his former star.

The opening voice-over introduces the city with a description that stresses its exoticism:

> This is Macao: a fabulous speck on the earth's surface, just off the coast of China, a thirty-five mile boat trip from Hong Kong. It is an ancient Portuguese colony, quaint and bizarre, the crossroads of the Far East, its population a mixture of all races and nationalities, mostly Chinese.

The description concludes with a statement that suggests Macao's similarity to cinema:

> Macao—often called the Monte Carlo of the Orient—has two faces: one calm and open; the other veiled and secret . . .

For Sternberg, the city has replaced the star as the primary vehicle for his exploration of cinema's basic principles, and the narration introduces its duality with costume references that imply mystery and inaccessibility. The description of the city is also reminiscent of Shanghai Lily, the veiled, enigmatic foreigner in *Shanghai Express* whose inaccessibility was signified, in part, by her costumes. Macao, like Lily, is "dressed" in elements of mise-en-scène that conceal its true identity and hint at its exoticism. Like the Shanghai of *The Shanghai Gesture,* and the Dietrich persona of his earlier films, Macao represents the unknown, the mysterious, the alluringly strange.

Sternberg "clothes" Macao in his familiar elements of mise-en-scène which act as impediments to the display function and accessibility of the photographic image. Once again, John Baxter refers to visual clutter and unreal atmosphere as evidence of Sternberg's contribution to the film.[19]

While Andrew Sarris considers Sternberg's contribution to *Macao* to have been minimal, he, too, cites various examples of Sternbergian style, including the murder of Bendix (shot through nets), and the chase across the bobbing floats.[20]

Jane Russell, while too sexually blatant to approach the enigmatic eroticism of Dietrich, creates an interesting character, and her costumes signify her complexity. She is introduced with a tilt shot that emphasizes her legs and is reminiscent of the introduction of the Dietrich character in *Dishonored*. Julie (Russell) is dressed in a costume that combines the obviousness of American sexuality with the mystery of Oriental style: she wears a two-piece dress that appears to have been purchased from two different hemispheres. The tight-fitting, décolleté bodice that accentuates her bustline is combined with a sarong-like skirt; together they stress her foreignness while maintaining her duality. After she is aided by Nick (Mitchum), who rescues her from the attack of a boorish American who has misread her signals as come-ons, she dons a straw Oriental hat, emphasizing her Eastern exoticism. Combining sexual frankness and deception (she casually lifts Nick's wallet during an embrace), Julie will, throughout the film, continue to embody contradiction. The night-club and gambling house in which she performs is owned by Halloran, and she affects a romantic/sexual interest in him in order to assist Nick in his efforts to avenge the murder of Trumble. Like many other Sternberg women, her role as a performer signifies her duality, and serves as a vehicle for disguise and deception. Other characters, as well, are in disguise, or, like some we have seen in other films, are hiding secrets. Nick is a fugitive from justice, Trumble is a detective disguised as a businessman, Halloran is a jewelry smuggler, and Halloran's cynical girlfriend, Margie (Gloria Grahame) participates in deception by helping Nick escape so that he can take her competition—Julie—away with him. In its attention to disguise as a costume metaphor for deception (used earlier in *Shanghai Express*, *Dishonored* and *Jet Pilot*), as well as in its transfer of the central object of mystery from star to city (seen previously in *The Shanghai Gesture*), *Macao*, while clearly not fully under Sternberg's control, shows evidence of the director's earlier work and concerns. As John Baxter has suggested, the film, which disowned by Sternberg, is "in the grand style of *The Shanghai Gesture*," and in an atmosphere and decor, is "clearly Sternberg's work."[21]

Julie (Jane Russell) in her East/West costume in *Macao*. (Museum of Modern Art Film Stills Archive)

8

Self-Reflexive Films: *The Last Command* and *The Saga of Anatahan*

Interestingly, Sternberg's most self-reflexive films appear early and late in his career. *The Last Command,* a silent film made in 1928, reflects the director's development as an artist, while *Anatahan,* his last film made in 1953, reflects his professional decline.

The Last Command (1928) is Sternberg's most blatantly self-reflexive film. It presents a richly drawn portrait of Hollywood, and introduces the director's concerns with the nature of cinema in the form of tensions centered around truth and illusion.

The story concerns a former Russian revolutionary who has come to Hollywood to direct motion pictures. The director, Andreyev (a Sternberg analogue played by William Powell) has decided to make a film about the Russian Revolution. In a bid for realism, Andreyev searches for the "perfect" person to cast in the role of the command-ing general. The discovery that the former grand duke Sergius (Emil Jannings) is working as an extra leads Andreyev to cast the now-broken old man in a role that recreates his actual past in Russia. The role-playing permits a lengthy flashback that gives Sternberg the opportunity to juxtapose "truth" (the subjective memory of the past) with illusion (Hollywood's interpretation of truth). The film-within-the-film allows Andreyev to better understand history through the illusory medium of film, and he ends up by praising the dying old man's patriotism, something he could not "see" while he was in-volved in the actuality of the revolution. Here Sternberg explores the often-deceptive nature of subjective reality as it contrasts with cinema's potential to present its own illusion of reality. In fact, Stern-berg was always more interested in the brand of truth that cinema could affect than he was in reality, and often expressed his disdain for "the fetish of authenticity."[1]

The opening title card, announcing the Hollywood of 1928 as the "Magic Empire of the twentieth century—the Mecca of the world," suggests Sternberg's attention both to Hollywood's attraction for

European artists (Murnau, Sjostrom and Stiller had already arrived as emigrés) and to the medium's potential for manipulating reality. The first images present Sternberg's multilayered approach to the question of truth and illusion. Andreyev looks at photographs (representations of reality not unlike the film image, a metaphor Sternberg also used in *The Blue Angel*) in an attempt to choose an appropriate actor to play the role of the commanding general in his current film. Andreyev, the former revolutionary, in his present position as Hollywood director, is treated like a king in this world of illusion. As many hands reach out to light his cigarette, obsequious assistants clamor to carry out his orders to hire the duke-turned-extra and "fit him into a general's uniform." This exchange of positions (the duke becomes an extra; the revolutionary becomes an autocratic "king") introduces Sternberg's concern with Hollywood's manipulation of truth, a concern explored throughout the film using the metaphor of Hollywood and its attempts to reproduce the illusion of reality. The director's order suggests that in this world of make-believe, men can be transformed—characters can be created—by the power of the director, who is capable of manipulating reality and impeding revelation through disguise or concealment.

The metaphor is elaborated upon as the former duke, now a dispirited extra willing to work for very little money, joins the "bread line of Hollywood" to receive the accoutrements of his role. In a scene that chronicles the construction of character through costume and makeup, Sergius approaches window after window, receiving accessories (boots, hat, sword) that will construct his new Hollywood character, while ironically recreating his past persona. Here Sternberg portrays Hollywood as the creator of illusion, a notion that forms the structural basis for *The Last Command*. The piles of uniforms from which his general's costume is assembled suggest the ease with which illusion can be ordered up; moreover, the costume dispenser tosses both general's and corporal's costumes with the same carelessness, emphasizing the leveling of rank among the anonymous Hollywood extras.

Sternberg advances the idea of character construction as Hollywood illusion by situating the next scene in a dressing room. As we have seen, the dressing room will be a favorite location for subsequent Sternberg characters, many of whom are performers; it will also become a recurring location for the inception of role-playing.

As his former power and individuality are reduced to the level of anonymous Hollywood extra by the indignities he suffers, Sergius continues to build his role by applying makeup. In an attempt to authenticate his costume, he produces his own medal, a token of loyalty and bravery actually given to him by the Czar. But the medal's authenticity is questioned by a fellow extra who suggests that it must have come from a "hock shop." The other extras taunt the old man, devaluing his sign of authenticity by placing the medal atop a prop bayonet and forcing Sergius to retrieve it. Later, the medal will again be used to explore the conflict between truth and illusion when its authenticity is questioned by the assistant director and then verified by the director.

While the nervously quivering Sergius applies his makeup before a dressing table mirror, he remembers his former life. The lengthy flashback which follows tells the story of the revolution, using the mirror to link the subjective reality of memory to the interpretative illusion of reality produced by cinema. Sternberg extends the metaphor of the mirror throughout the film by means of visual repetition.

Sergius (Emil Jannings) before the dressing table mirror in *The Last Command*. (Museum of Modern Art Film Stills Archive)

Shouting crowds and frames cluttered with moving people link the world of memory with the recreated world of Hollywood, while tracking shots of Russian troop inspections recur in studio dressing rooms where extras are reviewed by the director. Andrew Sarris points out the formal contrast between the two similar "troop review" scenes, noting how the difference between the direction of Sergius' lateral movement from left to right and Andreyev's "semi-vertical" movement from right to left create a kind of "visual versification."[2] In fact, the scenes are mirror images of one another, repeating, as Eileen Bowser has suggested, "the same movement in reverse."[3] The movement is repeated a third time by the camera, which files past the extras who stand at attention for the assistant director. Bowser also mentions another important use of the mirror. When Natacha (Evelyn Brent), the revolutionary spy, tries to shoot Sergius in the back, she fails because she has fallen in love with him.[4] Here, the mirror is used to reveal the truth to Sergius, who sees, in its reflection, Natacha's attempt to murder him. The mirror, therefore, serves to emphasize the deception that exists within the film's narrative and among its characters.

John Baxter points out that multiple layers of deception enrich the above scene. Alexander purposely turns his back on Natacha after seeing her pistol; Natacha, unable to kill Alexander, uses phony patriotism as her excuse.[5]

Deception, exposed in this scene by the mirror, is a favorite Sternberg motif. In later films it is realized through costume signs such as disguise, but in this film it is located in the major costume motif of role-playing. One of the major sartorial signifiers of role-playing in *The Last Command* is Sergius' greatcoat, an oversized sign of authority which the inhibited actor, according to Sternberg, used as refuge, a place in which to hide.[6]

The greatcoat (reminiscent of the doorman's coat in Murnau's *The Last Laugh,* and a sign of the expressionistic influence on the role of costume) becomes the link between Sergius' remembered past and attempts to recreate that past through Hollywood illusion. The association of his authority with the coat is reinforced by two incidents concerning an underling who covets the garment and tries it on, but is caught in the act by Sergius. Later, in the scene in which Sergius is stripped of his authority and humiliated by hordes of angry revolutionaries, the same underling tears the coat from Sergius' shoulders, proclaiming the shift in power with the cry: "We have been slaves too long. Now we are the masters!" This is an example of another kind of role-playing and one which betrays Sternberg's real feelings about revolution—that lust for power is unavoidably transferred from the privileged to the underprivileged. But the falseness of the coat as carrier of meaningful authority is emphasized later when the coat-snatcher, declaring that he wants Natacha, since she "goes with the coat," is summarily shot by a peasant who mocks such fraudulent authority. Sternberg's analysis of role-playing extends to delusion, as the underling mistakes the sign of authority (the coat) for actual authority, a delusion destroyed by the peasant who sees through it. Role-playing as deception is further emphasized by the characterizations of Andreyev and Natacha, both of whom begin as revolutionaries disguised as actors. Introduced in a shot that frames them in a window and resembles a photograph, the two are brought to the attention of Sergius by an assistant whose words reinforce the idea of role-playing as deception: "They are actors playing for the troops and their passports are in order—but our reports show they are revolutionists." When Sergius orders them to appear before him, his accusation further emphasizes the extent of their duality: "So you two are serving your country—by acting!" While the words seem judgmental and accusatory, Sternberg distinguishes between role-playing for a cause and play-acting at the expense of human life. When the czar insists on inspecting troops that are needed at the front, Sergius responds angrily, calling the poorly timed inspection a "show." The czar's request for a "staged" offensive at the front makes Sergius defiant. His reply ("My troops are not prepared for an offensive! I will not sacrifice them merely for the entertainment of the Czar!") reveals the general's true character.

Deception through role-playing is further emphasized in the actions of Natacha. She has not been completely successful as a Mata Hari, since her real affection and admiration for Sergius, inspired by his humanity towards his men and defiance of the czar, has made her unable to shoot him. But when his life is threatened by the takeover, she affects a hard-line approach by calling for his hanging in Petrograd. She insists that he be humiliated by forcing him to stoke the fire on the train which transports them there. While Sergius stokes the engine's fire, Natacha confesses her true feelings for the stunned, broken general. She admits that she has been play-acting in order to save his life, and gives him a string of pearls to buy his way out of Russia. When she believes that they are being observed, she affects an about-face, turning on Sergius and expressing her passion for a man she does not know so that Sergius can make his escape. After Sergius jumps from the train, a bridge collapses, sending the train and its passengers, including Natacha, to an icy grave. The shock of this sight is what apparently has contributed to Sergius' nervous head-shaking. The flashback ends with Sergius still at the mirror applying makeup as the title card informs us how "the backwash of a tortured nation had carried still another extra to Hollywood." The assistant director files past the hordes of extras at their dressing tables, and when he reaches Sergius places a medal on his costume. He informs him that the director has an important part for him which will require that he "look nice." The despotic assistant director comments on the importance of authenticity and realism in creating a role when he chides a makeup artist for his ineffectiveness: "Is that beard supposed to be Russian? It looks like an ad for cough drops!" The line further emphasizes Sternberg's attention to questions of truth and illusion, signified here by the conflict between historical accuracy and the attempt to recreate it through makeup. But the assistant director's apparent concern for veracity proves superficial. When Sergius switches the position of his medal, citing history as his source ("In Russia, that was worn on the left side. I know, because I was a general"), the assistant director contradicts him with his own source of accuracy: "I've made twenty Russian pictures. You can't tell me anything about Russia." Sternberg here pits the subjective reality of the general's memory against the illusion of reality created by cinema, commenting on the power of the illusion to obscure the truth. But the director, himself a Russian, cannot accept the illusion of reality since he knows it is false, and he returns the medal to its rightful position on Sergius' uniform.

After supervising Sergius's costuming, Andreyev comments on the similarity between the illusion of reality produced by cinema and the subjective reality produced by memory: "The same coat, the same uniform, the same man—only the times have changed." Hollywood illusion begins as lights are adjusted, actors take their places, and wind machines recreate the Russia of the revolution. Andreyev orders the Russian national anthem played, and Sergius, once again in his greatcoat, begins to believe the illusion. He "sees" crowds of revolutionaries swarm over Hollywood barbed wire, as Sternberg literalizes the illusion with the cinematic trick of superimposition. The crew turns into hordes of frantic people, as Sergius warns them of their fate: "People of Russia—you are being led by traitors—we must win or Russia will perish!" Finally, the old man dies in the director's arms, still unaware of the distinction between truth (the past) and illusion (role-playing and filmmaking), and asking whether they have won. The director's reply, "Yes, you have won," marks the triumph of truth over illusion and reinforces Sternberg's faith in the ability of cinema to produce an illusion of reality often more skillful in revealing truth than reality itself. For when the assistant director expresses his sorrow ("Tough luck! That guy was a great actor"), Andreyev's reply ("He was more than a great actor—he was a great man") indicates his understanding of the truth of Sergius' real character. Here the Sternberg analogue, the director, has arrived at a truth not approachable without the medium of film, since it is the recreation of history through cinema that has provided the insight. Kevin Brownlow has considered the director's response a flaw in the film's narrative, since Andreyev could not have known about the general's true personality, having met him only once and never having seen Natacha again before she died.[7] Sternberg defends the "flaw" by saying that Andreyev's statement is "based on his observation of Sergius' performance in the trenches in the studio."[8] Sternberg's defense makes more sense in terms of the film's broad investigation of the nature of cinema's potential. The film ends with a pull-back dolly that reveals the equipment responsible for creating illusion (the lights and cameras) and acts as a visual exclamation point to a story whose truth is ultimately revealed by the power of a medium that can create the "illusion of authenticity." This illusion is often more capable of approaching truth, according to Sternberg, than the reality obscured by subjectivity or hidden within individual memory.

The Saga of Anatahan (1953) was Sternberg's final film and, perhaps, the director's fullest effort to exercise total control over his medium. Most outstanding as a film which resists the "realism" of cinema, both in substance and in style, *Anatahan*'s attention to costume signs is, for practical reasons, less in evidence than in earlier Sternberg films. However, the film focuses on familiar Sternbergian themes and tensions, and serves as a fitting summary of the concerns of earlier works.

Based on a novel by Michiro Maruyama, who was writing about a personal experience, and also on newspaper and *Life* magazine accounts, the story concerns a group of Japanese sailors marooned on an isolated Pacific island. Unwilling to believe that the war had ended, they decide to remain on the island and maintain their warlike stance against the unseen American enemy. While on the island they meet the beautiful Keiko (Akemi Negishi), first just "another survivor . . . then female . . . then woman—the only woman on earth," as Sternberg's voice-over narration reveals. Their isolation and her irresistible beauty become a fatal mixture. Desire and passion divide the sailors, and cause the deaths of four of the men through jealousies and power plays. The film ends with Keiko leaving the island herself and later convincing the remaining sailors, through correspondence from their families in Japan, to do the same.

Sternberg was attracted to the project because he was able to make it under what he termed "almost ideal conditions."[9] Working entirely in a studio in Japan, Sternberg was given complete autonomy, an arrangement he had not had since *The Devil Is A Woman*. In an interview with Peter Bogdanovich, Sternberg said he had gone to Japan precisely because he thought he could have complete freedom there.[10] The film's titles state that *Anatahan* was "filmed in a studio specially constructed for the purpose in Kyoto, the ancient capital of Japan." John Baxter reports how Sternberg's construction in Kyoto of a totally artificial setting in an aircraft hangar, cluttered with upended swamp tree roots and vines and sprayed with aluminum paint, allowed the director to create his "most claustrophobic work."[11]

In an interview with Herman Weinberg, Sternberg explained his desire to work in a studio rather than on location on the island of Anatahan.

> Anatahan is an island located two thousand kilometers from Japan, half-way from the Philippines. Anyway, it was impossible to shoot a picture there: it's a jungle. But if I did not work on location, it was on purpose. I prefer to work in a studio. Outside, the tourists get in my way. I like to be comfortable; too bad if the actors are not.[12]

But more important, perhaps, than the desire to hide from tourists was the opportunity to exercise control over every aspect of production, including the construction of a mini-universe which, though it resembled the jungle atmosphere of a Pacific island, was Sternberg's own artistic creation. As Sternberg boasted:

> You have seen *The Docks of New York;* well, the film was made in a studio. I recreated China in a studio for *Shanghai Express*, for *The Shanghai Gesture*, for *Macao*. . . . Everything is artificial in *Anatahan*, even the clouds are painted and the plane is a toy. This film is my own creation.[13]

As part of his plan to exercise complete control, Sternberg chose nonfilm actors (several had worked in Kabuki theater) to portray his characters. Working with people unaccustomed to acting in films enabled Sternberg to direct them rather closely, and he returned to a relationship similar in many ways to that which he had had with Dietrich. At times, the actors appear to have been directed even in their facial expressions, and many of their looks seem posed and artificial. As if this were not enough for Sternberg to prove his artistic despotism, the director added his own voice-over narration to the Japanese dialogue, providing a second layer of subjectivity to Sternberg's already subjective visuals.

Most interesting about *Anatahan* is its use of Sternberg's opposition to realism as an organizing principle for the film's narrative and thematic concerns. For the characters stranded on the island, there is a constant tension between truth (the actuality of the war's end) and illusion (their resistance to believing such a truth), a tension that mirrors Sternberg's own resistance to a medium that signals "realism." Like Sternberg, the survivors create their own hermetically sealed microcosm of fantasy, preferring to live in a world of illusion and falling prey to a woman who leaves them. At one point, Sternberg's narration expresses the obvious parallel between Keiko and Dietrich: "When a woman threatens to leave, this has a considerable effect on a man, even if she's not the only woman on earth." When the narration says that "this lonely island was our whole world," it could be referring to cinema as well as to Anatahan. Both locations provide fertile atmospheres for the continuing struggle between life and art.

Due to the action's restriction to an isolated island in the Pacific, Sternberg could not, even if he had wanted to do so, pay a significant amount of attention to costume signs. Even Sternberg would have been hard-pressed to find justification in this film for the kind of costume changes that many of his earlier films required. Still, *Anatahan* contains some references to costume that betray Sternberg's unflagging interest in the subject.

The opposition in the film is between truth (both the truth inherent in the photographic verisimilitude of the film image as well as the truth or reality of the war's conclusion) and illusion (both the illusion of a real world created by Sternberg's art as well as the unreal world of illusion that the film's characters create and inhabit). Sternberg uses costume as both a sign of that opposition and a reflection of its shifting emphases. As the film progresses, the collective protagonist (i.e., the sailors) changes costume only three times. Clothed, at first, in their tattered uniforms, the sailors then change to "environmental" garments (grass, burlap and other "natural" materials), and finally to costumes fashioned by Keiko from a parachute she discovers in the wreckage of a plane. In Sternberg's sign system the uniforms represent a hierarchy imposed by civilization on men who conform to its rules. The "environmental" costumes indicate adaptation to a world that does not honor rigidly imposed societal hierarchies, preferring to make its own rules based on needs and power plays. The parachute costumes suggest a recognition of the existence of the outside world. It is the first real sign of their acceptance of it, an acceptance that prefigures their eventual escape from the island and their return to civilization.

The Last Command and *Anatahan* represent a major shift in the director's point of view during his career from optimism to despair.

Keiko (Akemi Negishi) and the sailors in their "environmental" costumes in *The Saga of Anatahan*. (Photofest)

If *The Last Command* explores cinema's potential to reveal truth through the creation of an "illusion of authenticity" more capable of approaching truth than the reality obscured by subjectivity or selective memory, then *Anatahan* acknowledges its failure. Whereas *The Last Command* looks forward to a developing aesthetic and potentially rich career, *Anatahan* reflects back on their disappointments. As Andrew Sarris has suggested, "Nothing really happens in *Anatahan;* every incident is filtered through a thick veil of remembrance and regret."[14] *The Last Command* is Sternberg's preface to a battle between the developing artist and the medium in which he worked; *Anatahan* is his epilogue to its scars.

Notes

Chapter 1. Introduction

1. Dale McConathy and Diana Vreeland, *Hollywood Costume: Glamour! Glitter! Romance!* (New York: Harry N. Abrams, 1976), 21.

2. See Charles Eckert, "The Carole Lombard in Macy's Window," *Quarterly Review of Film Studies,* Winter 1978; Maureen Turim, "Gentlemen Consume Blondes," *Wide Angle* 1, no. 1 (1979) and "Designing Women: The Emergence of the New Sweetheart Line," *Wide Angle* 6, no. 2 (1984); Jane Gaines and Charlotte Herzog, "Hildy Johnson and the 'Man-Tailored Suit': The Comedy of Inequality," *Film Reader 5,* 1982; and Jane Gaines: "The Queen Christina Tie-Ups: Convergence of Show Window and Screen," *Quarterly Review of Film and Video* 2, no. 1 (1989). The recent anthology *Fabrications: Costume and the Female Body,* ed. Jane Gaines and Charlotte Herzog (New York: Routledge, 1990), is an excellent collection of essays centered around the assumption that woman as a "constructed" image in films is largely a product, not only of film technique and spectatorship, but also of the way in which women's bodies are presented and adorned. Several of the essays listed above are reprinted in this volume, and there are others that collectively cover a good deal of ground in reevaluating and organizing feminist theory and cultural study in their relationship to costume practice.

3. See Gaylyn Studlar, *In the Realm of Pleasure: Von Sternberg, Dietrich and the Masochistic Aesthetic* (Urbana and Chicago: University of Illinois Press, 1988). Studlar reevaluates feminist theories of spectatorship through an investigation of Gilles Deleuze's theory of masochism and its theoretical application to the subversive potential of pleasure offered in classical Hollywood cinema. In her analysis, Studlar makes a convincing case for the use of costume in Sternberg's films as crucial in the production of pleasure for both male and female spectators. It thus challenges earlier, oedipal interpretations of female representation (Freudian and Lacanian).

4. Roland Barthes, "The Diseases of Costume," in *Critical Essays,* trans. Richard Howard (Evanston: Northwestern University Press, 1972), 46.

5. Ibid., 44–45.

6. Josef von Sternberg, *Fun in a Chinese Laundry* (New York: Collier Books, 1965), 16.

7. Ibid., 17.

8. John Baxter, *The Cinema of Josef von Sternberg* (New York: A. S. Barnes, 1971), 15.

9. Ibid., 11.

10. Edith Head and Paddy Calistro, *Edith Head's Hollywood* (New York: E. P. Dutton, 1983), 28.

11. David A. Cook, *A History of Narrative Film* (New York: W. W. Norton, 1981), 271.

12. John Baxter, as quoted in Cook, 271.

13. Margaret Bailey, *Those Glorious, Glamour Years* (Secaucus, N.J.: Citadel Press, 1982), 7.

14. Sternberg, 239.

15. Sternberg, "Introduction" to the published script *The Blue Angel* (London: Lorrimer, 1968), 11.

16. David Chierichetti, *Hollywood Costume Design* (New York: Harmony, 1976), 50.

17. Ibid., 42.

18. Jurij Lotman, *Semiotics of Cinema*, trans. Mark E. Suino (Ann Arbor: University of Michigan, 1981), 18.

19. Ibid., 20.

20. Joyce Rheuben, "Joseph von Sternberg: The Scientist and the Vamp," *Sight and Sound,* Winter 1972–73.

21. Josef von Sternberg, as quoted in an interview with Philippe Esnault and Michele Firk, *Positif* 37–38 (1961), reprinted in Weinberg, 133.

22. Andrew Sarris, *The Films of Josef von Sternberg* (New York: Museum of Modern Art, 1966), 46.

Chapter 2. A Developing Aesthetic

1. Andrew Sarris, *The Films of Josef von Sternberg* (New York: Museum of Modern Art, 1966), 11.

2. Marcel Oms, "Joseph von Sternberg," in *Sternberg,* ed. Peter Baxter (London: British Film Institute, 1980), 69.

3. Josef von Sternberg, *Fun in a Chinese Laundry* (New York: Collier, 1965), 164.

4. John Baxter, *The Cinema of Josef von Sternberg* (New York: A. S. Barnes, 1971), 16.

5. Edith Head, as quoted in Margaret Bailey, *Those Glorious, Glamour Years* (Secaucus, N.J.: Citadel, 1982), 137.

6. John Baxter, 22.

7. Oms, 62.

8. Eileen Bowser, "Underworld," in *Film Notes,* ed. Eileen Bowser (New York: Museum of Modern Art, 1969), 66.

Chapter 3. Role-Playing and Performance as Layering

1. Peter Wollen, *Signs and Meaning in the Cinema* (Bloomington: Indiana UP, 1969), 136.

2. Ibid., 137.

3. Jurij Lotman, *Semiotics of Cinema*, trans. Mark E. Suino (Ann Arbor: University of Michigan, 1981), 21.

4. Josef von Sternberg, *Fun in a Chinese Laundry* (New York: Collier, 1965), 97.

5. Ibid., 227.

6. Ibid., 230.

7. Ibid., 231.

8. Phillipe Roberts-Jones, *Beyond Time and Place: Non-Realist Painting in the Nineteenth Century* (London: Oxford UP, 1978), 166.

9. John Baxter, *The Cinema of Josef von Sternberg* (New York: A. S. Barnes, 1971), 68–69.

10. Andrew Sarris, *The Films of Josef Von Sternberg* (New York: Museum of Modern Art, 1966), 12.

11. Frank McConnell, *The Spoken Seen* (Baltimore: Johns Hopkins UP, 1975), 179.

12. Alexander Walker, *The Celluloid Sacrifice* (New York: Hawthorn, 1967), 85.

13. Ibid., 84.

14. James Laver, *A Concise History of Costume* (London: Thames and Hudson, 1969), 127.

15. Anne Hollander, *Seeing Through Clothes* (New York: Avon, 1980), 445.

16. Andrew Sarris, "The Cinema of Josef von Sternberg," repr. in Herman Weinberg, *Josef von Sternberg* (New York: E. P. Dutton, 1967), 186.

17. Sternberg, 91.

18. Hollander, 133.

19. Sarris, *The Films of Josef von Sternberg*, 25.

20. Ibid.

21. J. C. Flugel, *The Psychology of Clothes* (New York: International Universities, 1930), 20.

22. Lawrence Langner, *The Importance of Wearing Clothes* (New York: Hastings House, 1959), 44.

23. Ibid., 46.

24. Ibid., 235.

25. Hollander, 218.

26. Heinrich Mann, as quoted in Weinberg, 51.

27. Hollander, 214.

28. Alan Casty, as quoted in McConnell, 178.

29. Peter Baxter, "On the Naked Thighs of Miss Dietrich," *Wide Angle* 2, no. 2 (1978): 22.

30. This is a variant ending. The German version ends with Rath dead at his classroom desk.

31. James Laver, *Modesty in Dress* (Boston: Houghton Mifflin, 1969), 13.

32. Anne Hollander, *Seeing Through Clothes* (New York: Avon, 1980), 83.

33. Ibid., 84.

34. E. Ann Kaplan, *Women and Film* (New York: Methuen, 1983), 53.

35. Hollander, 86.

36. Ibid.

37. Ibid.

38. Laver, 11.

39. Alexander Lowen, "In Defense of Modesty," in *Dimensions of Dress and Adornment*, ed. Gurel and Beeson (Dubuque: Kendall/Hunt, 1975), 102.

40. Ibid.

41. Kaplan, 56.

42. Robin Wood, "Venus de Marlene," *Film Comment*, March/April 1978: 60.

43. Lowen, 104.

44. Wood, 63.

45. Stefan Sharff, *The Elements of Cinema* (New York: Columbia UP, 1982), 119.

46. Bill Nichols, *Ideology and the Image* (Bloomington: Indiana UP, 1981), 125.

47. Ibid., 125.

48. Roland Barthes, *Mythologies,* trans. Annette Lavers (New York: Hill and Wang, 1972), 84.

49. Ibid.

50. Claire Johnston, "Myths of Women in the Cinema," as quoted in Kaplan, 50.

51. Robin Wood, "Venus de Marlene," *Film Comment,* March/April 1978: 61.

52. Ibid.

53. Ibid.

54. Joyce Rheuben, "The Scientist and the Vamp," *Sight and Sound,* Winter 1972–73: 37.

55. Nichols, 123–24.

56. Kaplan, 53.

57. Carolyn Heilbrun, *Toward a Recognition of Androgyny* (New York: W. W. Norton, 1973), x–xi.

58. Thomas Rosenmeyer, "Tragedy and Religion: *The Bacchae,*" quoted in Heilbrun, xi.

59. Susan Gubar, "Blessings in Disguise: Cross-Dressing as Re-Dressing for Female Modernists," *Massachusetts Review,* Autumn 1981: 478.

60. Ibid.

61. Ibid., 481.

62. Rebecca Bell-Metereau, *Hollywood Androgyny* (New York: Columbia UP, 1985), 19.

63. Kaplan, 57.

64. Ibid., 50.

65. Ibid., 53.

66. Claire Johnston, "Myths of Women in the Cinema," repr. in *Women and the Cinema,* ed. Karyn Kay and Gerald Peary (New York: E. P. Dutton, 1974), 411.

67. Wood, 63.

68. Ibid.

Chapter 4. Deception, Spying, and Disguise

1. Josef von Sternberg, *Fun in a Chinese Laundry* (New York: Collier, 1965), 257.

2. Anne Hollander, *Seeing Through Clothes* (New York: Avon, 1980), 262.

3. John Baxter, *The Cinema of Josef von Sternberg* (New York: A. S. Barnes, 1971), 84.

4. Oto Bihalji-Merin, *Great Masks* (New York: Harry N. Abrams, 1970), 7.

5. Sternberg, 92.

6. Bihalji-Merin, 9.

7. Andrew Sarris, *The Films of Josef von Sternberg* (New York: Museum of Modern Art, 1966).

8. Joyce Rheuben, "The Scientist and the Vamp," *Sight and Sound* 42, no. 1 (1972/73): 39.

9. Alexander Walker, *The Celluloid Sacrifice* (New York: Hawthorn, 1967), 90.

10. Ethan Mordden, *Movie Star* (New York: St. Martin's, 1983), 109.

11. Walker, 90.

12. O. O. Green, "Six Films of Josef von Sternberg," *Movie* 13 (Summer 1965): 28.

13. Richard Dyer, *Stars* (London: British Film Institute, 1979), 146.

14. Ibid., 147.

15. Green, 28.

16. Leo Braudy, *The World In A Frame* (Garden City, N.Y.: Doubleday, 1976), 193.

17. David Chierichetti, *Hollywood Costume Design* (New York: Harmony, 1976), 55.

18. Sarris, 32.

19. Ibid., 31.

20. Baxter, 99.

21. Ibid., 91.

22. Rheuben, 35.

23. Maureen Turim, "Gentlemen Consume Blondes," *Wide Angle* 1, no. 1 (1979): 58.

24. Wendy Cooper, *Hair* (New York: Stein and Day, 1971), 75.

25. Henry Wadsworth Longfellow, as quoted in Cooper, 75.

26. Dale McConathy and Diana Vreeland, *Hollywood Costume: Glamour! Glitter! Romance!* (New York: Harry N. Abrams, 1976), 127.

27. In fact, woman's costume in films has traditionally been associated with her otherness. She has appeared as black widow spider, Venus fly trap and vampire in costumes which express her deadly danger.

28. Alison Lurie, *The Language of Clothes* (New York: Random House, 1981), 239.

29. John Belton, dissertation comments. For Sybil DelGaudio, "Clothing Signification in the Films of Joseph von Sternberg," (Ph.D. Columbia University, 1986).

30. Rheuben, 38.

31. Hollander, 342.

32. Ibid., 365.

33. Ibid., 385.

34. John Kobal, *Marlene Dietrich* (New York: E. P. Dutton, 1968), 60.

35. Baxter, 95.

36. Lurie, 25.

37. Molly Haskell, *From Reverence to Rape* (New York: Holt, Rinehart, Winston, 1973), 112.

38. Walker, 90.

39. Peter Wollen, *Signs and Meanings in the Cinema* (Bloomington, Indiana UP, 1969), 136.

40. Bailey, 356.

41. Ibid., 359.

42. Ibid.

43. Baxter, 80.

44. Ibid., 67.

45. Ibid., 9.

46. Joseph von Sternberg, as quoted in Charles Silver, *Marlene Dietrich* (New York: Pyramid, 1974), 29.

47. Bailey, 192.

48. K. M. Lester and B. V. Oerke, *Accessories of Dress* (Peoria, Ill.: Manual Arts, 1940), 61.

49. Walker, 85.

50. Bailey, 112.

51. Lawrence Langner, *The Importance of Wearing Clothes* (New York: Hastings House, 1959), 316.

52. Ibid., 317.

53. Ibid., 326.

54. Sarris, 45.

55. Sternberg, 271.

56. Sarris, 45.

57. Marcel Oms, "Josef von Sternberg," in *Sternberg*, ed. Peter Baxter (London: British Film Institute, 1980), 75.

58. John Baxter, 134–35.

59. Sternberg, 271.

60. John Baxter, 135.

61. Ibid., 162.

62. Sternberg, 282.

63. John Baxter, 162.

64. Ezra Goodman, as quoted in John Baxter, 163.

65. Sternberg, 282.

66. Ibid.

67. John Baxter, 165–66.

68. Sternberg interview by Peter Bogdanovich, "Encounters with Josef von Sternberg," *Movie* 13 (Summer 1965): 25.

69. Luc Moullet, "Saint Janet," in *Sternberg*, ed. Peter Baxter (London: British Film Institute, 1980), 50.

Chapter 5. Stylization as Distance

1. Josef von Sternberg, *Fun in a Chinese Laundry* (New York: Collier, 1965), 293.

2. Peter Wollen, *Signs and Meaning in the Cinema* (Bloomington: Indiana UP, 1969), 137.

3. Ibid., 136.

4. Ibid., 137.

5. Ibid.

6. Jack Babuscio, "Camp and the Gay Sensibility," in *Gays and Film*, ed. Richard Dyer (London: British Film Institute, 1977), 51.

7. Susan Sontag, "Notes on Camp," in *Against Interpretation* (New York: Dell, 1961), 285.

8. Ibid., 277.

9. Babuscio, 51.

10. Sontag, 281.

11. Babuscio, 44.

12. Ibid., 40.

13. O. O. Green, "Six Films of Josef von Sternberg," *Movie* 13 (Summer 1965): 28.

14. Herman Weinberg, *Josef von Sternberg* (New York: E. P. Dutton, 1967), 194.

15. Review of *Shanghai Express* in *Vanity Fair*, as quoted in Sternberg, 262.

16. Bardesch and Barsillach, as quoted in Sternberg, 260.

17. Barbuscio, 40.

18. Sontag, 281.

19. Andrew Sarris, *The Films of Josef von Sternberg* (New York: Museum of Modern Art, 1966), 31.

20. Babuscio, 50.

21. Ibid.

22. Sontag, 277.

23. Sternberg, 228.

24. Rebecca Bell-Metereau, *Hollywood Androgyny* (New York: Columbia UP, 1985), 103.

25. Sternberg, 247.

26. Ibid.

27. Adolph Zukor, as quoted in Sheridan Morley, *Marlene Dietrich* (New York: McGraw-Hill, 1976), 39.

28. Edith Head and Paddy Calistro, *Edith Head's Hollywood* (New York: E. P. Dutton, 1983), 19.

29. Margaret Bailey, *Those Glorious, Glamour Years* (Secaucus, N.J.: Citadel, 1982), 247.

30. Bell-Metereau, 70.

31. Susan Gubar, "Blessings in Disguise: Cross Dressing as Re-Dressing for Female Modernists," *The Massachusetts Review* 22, no. 3 (Autumn 1981): 478.

32. Simone de Beauvoir, as quoted in Gubar, 479.

33. Ibid.

34. Claire Johnston, "Myths of Women in the Cinema," *Women and the Cinema,* ed. Karyn Kay and Gerald Peary (New York: E. P. Dutton, 1977), 410.

35. Ibid.

36. Claire Johnston, "Women's Cinema As Counter Cinema," *Notes on Women's Cinema* (London: Society for Education in Film and Television), 28.

37. Laura Mulvey, "Visual Pleasure and Narrative Cinema," *Women and the Cinema* (New York: E. P. Dutton, 1977), 422.

38. Ibid.

39. Ibid., 423.

40. Bill Nichols, *Ideology and the Image* (Bloomington: Indiana UP, 1981), 123.

41. Sarris, 29.

42. Joan Riviere, "Womanliness as a Masquerade," *Psychoanalysis and Female Sexuality,* ed. Hendrik M. Ruitenbeek (New Haven, Conn.: College and UP Services), 210.

43. Jacques Lacan as quoted by the *Cahiers* critics in "Morocco," *Sternberg,* ed. Peter Baxter (London: British Film Institute, 1980), 82.

44. *Cahiers* critics, "Morocco," 82.

45. C. A. Lejeune, review of *Morocco* in *The Observer,* quoted in Morley, 41.

46. Robin Wood, "Venus de Marlene," *Film Comment* 14, no. 2 (March/April 1978): 63.

47. Morley, 65.

48. Sternberg, 267.

49. Sternberg, as quoted in Weinberg, 63.

50. Sarris, 40.

51. John Baxter, *The Cinema of Josef von Sternberg* (New York: A. S. Barnes, 1971), 122.

52. John Kobal, *Marlene Dietrich* (London: Studio Vista, 1968), 93.

53. Fritz Lang, as quoted in Kobal, 93.

54. Sternberg, 267.

55. Josef von Sternberg, as quoted in Sarris, 41.

56. Weinberg, 65.

57. Ibid.

58. Josef von Sternberg, as quoted in Sarris, 41.

59. Sternberg, 266.

60. Weinberg, 64.

61. Sarris, 42.

62. Eileen Bowser and Richard Griffith, "The Devil Is A Woman," in *Film Notes,* ed. Eileen Bowser (New York: Museum of Modern Art, 1969), 97.

63. Sarris, 42.

64. Ibid.

65. Patrick Bade, *Femme Fatale* (New York: Mayflower, 1979), 8.

66. Ibid., 11–12.

67. Ibid., 12.

68. Henri Agel, as quoted in Weinberg, 216.

69. Kobal, 92.

70. Sarris, 42.

71. Cecelia Ager, as quoted in Sarris, 42.

72. Bailey, 301.

73. Donald Spoto, *Falling in Love Again* (Boston: Little Brown, 1985), 81.

74. David Chierichetti, *Hollywood Costume Design* (New York: Harmony, 1976), 55.

75. Marlene Dietrich, as quoted in Spoto, 81.

76. Chierichetti, 55.

77. Dale McConathy and Diana Vreeland, *Hollywood Costume: Glamour! Glitter! Romance!* (New York: Harry N. Abrams, 1976), 124.

78. Josef von Sternberg, "The von Sternberg Principle," in *Sternberg,* ed. Peter Baxter (London: British Film Institute, 1980), 52.

79. Sternberg, "The von Sternberg Principle," in Peter Baxter, 53.

80. Ibid.

81. Ibid.

82. Ibid., 54.

83. Weinberg, 82.

84. Sternberg, "The von Sternberg Principle," in Peter Baxter, 53.

85. John Baxter, 129.

86. Josef von Sternberg, as quoted in the interview with Philippe Esnault and Michele Firk in *Positif,* 37–38 (1961), reprinted in Weinberg, 124.

Chapter 6. Sternberg vs. History

1. Title card, *The Scarlet Empress.*

2. Robin Wood, "*The Scarlet Empress:* The Play of Light and Shade," in *Personal Views: Explorations in Film* (London: Gordon Fraser, 1976), 99.

3. Anne Hollander, "The 'Gatsby Look' and Other Costume Movie Blunders," *New York* 7, no. 21 (27 May 1974): 58.

4. Walter Plunkett, as quoted in Margaret Bailey, *Those Glorious, Glamour Years* (Secaucus, N.J.: Citadel, 1982), 260.

5. Travis Banton, as quoted in Ruth Rankin, "Undraping Hollywood," *Photoplay* 45, no. 3 (Feb. 1934): 37.

6. William Gaines, "Hollywood Snubs Paris," *Photoplay* 45, no. 5 (April 1934): 48.

7. Travis Banton, as quoted in Bailey, 297.

8. John Baxter, *Hollywood in the Thirties* (New York: Warner, 1970), 46.

9. Leon Barsacq, *Caligari's Cabinet and Other Grand Illusions* (Boston: New York Graphic Society, 1976), 62.

10. Josef von Sternberg, *Fun in a Chinese Laundry* (New York: Collier, 1965), 265.

11. Ibid.

12. Ibid.

13. Rosalind Shaffer, "Catherine To Be More Colorful Than Authentic," *Daily News*, 19 Nov. 1933, p. 21.

14. Richard Watts, Jr., rev. of *The Scarlet Empress, New York Herald Tribune,* 15 Sept. 1934: 16.

15. André Sennwald, rev. of *The Scarlet Empress, New York Times,* 15 Sept. 1934, p. 26.

16. Rev. of *The Scarlet Empress* in *Time Magazine,* as quoted in Homer Dickens, *The Films of Marlene Dietrich* (New York: Citadel, 1968), 97.

17. André Sennwald, rev. of *Catherine the Great, New York Times,* 15 Feb. 1934, p. 21.

18. Richard Watts, Jr., rev. of *Catherine the Great, New York Herald Tribune,* 15 Feb. 1934, p. 18.

19. Hollander, 59.

20. Ruth Turner Wilcox, *The Mode in Costume* (New York: Scribner, 1949), 197.

21. William Gaines, 49.

22. Rev. of *The Scarlet Empress,* London *Times,* 10 May 1934, p. 41.

23. Sternberg, 266.

24. Ibid.

25. Tom Flinn, *"The Scarlet Empress," Velvet Light Trap* 16 (Fall 1976): 6.

26. As Bazin refers to cinema's inherent "realism" in "The Ontology of the Photographic Image" in *What Is Cinema?* vol. 1 (Berkeley: Univ. of California, 1971), 9–16.

27. Henri Langlois, as quoted in Herman Weinberg, *Josef von Sternberg* (New York: E. P. Dutton, 1967), 62.

28. G. W. Pabst, as quoted in Weinberg, 63.

29. Andrew Sarris, *The Films of Josef von Sternberg* (New York: Museum of Modern Art, 1966), 39.

30. Ibid.

31. Ibid.

32. Leo Braudy, *The World in a Frame* (New York: Doubleday, 1976), 88.

33. Ibid., 90.

34. Title card, *The Scarlet Empress.*

35. Wood, 108.

36. Ibid., 101.

37. Ibid.

38. Ibid., 102.

39. Rheuben, 40.

40. Wood, 112.

41. TItli card, *The Scarlet Empress.*

42. David Chierichetti, *Hollywood Costume Design* (New York: Harmony, 1976), 55.

43. Travis Banton, as quoted in Bailey, 297.

44. Bailey, 297.

45. Henri Troyat, *Catherine the Great* (New York: E. P. Dutton, 1980), 62.

46. Title card, *The Scarlet Empress.*

47. O. O. Green (Raymond Durgnat), "Six Films of Josef von Sternberg," *Movie* 13 (Summer 1965): 29.

48. Rheuben, 40.

49. Wood, 112.

50. Sternberg, 172–73.

51. Michael Korda, *Charmed Lives* (New York: Avon, 1979), 122.

52. Sternberg, 172.

53. Korda, 124.

54. Trade press, as quoted in John Baxter, *The Cinema of Josef von Sternberg* (London: A. S. Barnes, 1971), 137.

55. Josef von Sternberg, interviewed in *The Epic That Never Was*, produced by the BBC, 1966.

56. John Armstrong, as quoted in Weinberg, 69.

57. John Armstrong, interviewed in *The Epic That Never Was.*

Chapter 7. The City as Cinema

1. Herman Weinberg, *Joseph von Sternberg* (New York: E. P. Dutton, 1967), 70.

2. John Baxter, *The Cinema of Josef von Sternberg* (New York: A. S. Barnes, 1971), 156.

3. Josef von Sternberg, *Fun in a Chinese Laundry* (New York: Collier, 1965), 278.

4. Bosley Crowther, rev. of *The Shanghai Gesture*, *The New York Times*, 26 Dec. 1941, p. 21.

5. Opening titles in *The Shanghai Gesture*, 1941.

6. Frank Krutnik, "*The Shanghai Gesture:* The Exotic and Melodrama," *Wide Angle* 4, no. 2 (1980): 41.

7. Ibid., 38.

8. Ibid., 41.

9. Louis Audibert, "The Flash of the Look," in *Sternberg*, ed. Peter Baxter (London: British Film Institute, 1980), 101.

10. Marcel Oms, "Josef von Sternberg," in *Sternberg*, ed. Peter Baxter, 77.

11. John Baxter, 156.

12. O. O. Green, "Six Films of Josef von Sternberg," *Movie* 13 (Summer 1965): 31.

13. Henri Agel, "Josef von Sternberg," in *Les grandes cineastes* (Paris: 1959), reprinted in Weinberg, 216.

14. Andrew Sarris, *The Films of Josef von Sternberg* (New York: Museum of Modern Art, 1966), 50.

15. Ibid.

16. Josef von Sternberg, as quoted in Weinberg, 244.

17. Sternberg, 283.

18. Weinberg, 209.

19. John Baxter, 169.

20. Sarris, 53.
21. John Baxter, 167.

Chapter 8. Self-Reflexive Films

1. Kevin Brownlow, *The Parade's Gone By* (Berkeley: University of California, 1968), 202.

2. Andrew Sarris, *The Films of Josef von Sternberg* (New York: Museum of Modern Art, 1966), 18.

3. Eileen Bowser, "The Last Command," in *Film Notes,* ed. Eileen Bowser (New York: Museum of Modern Art, 1969), 71.

4. Ibid.

5. John Baxter, *The Cinema of Josef von Sternberg* (London: A. S. Barnes, 1971), 49.

6. Josef von Sternberg, *Fun in a Chinese Laundry* (New York: Collier, 1965), 130.

7. Brownlow, 197.

8. Josef von Sternberg, as quoted in Brownlow, 203.

9. Sternberg, *Fun in a Chinese Laundry,* 283.

10. Sternberg, interviewed by Peter Bogdanovich, as reported in "Encounters with Josef von Sternberg," *Movie* 13 (Summer 1965): 25.

11. Baxter, 174.

12. Sternberg, as quoted in an interview with Philippe Esnault and Michele Firk, *Positif,* 37–38 (1961), reprinted in Herman Weinberg, *Josef von Sternberg* (New York: E. P. Dutton, 1967), 125.

13. Ibid.

14. Sarris, 54.

Bibliography

Magazine or Journal Articles about and Interviews with Josef von Sternberg

Ager, Cecelia. "Optics on Roller Bearings." *Variety,* 8 May 1935.

Baxter, Peter. "On the Naked Thighs of Miss Dietrich." *Wide Angle* 2, no. 2 (1978).

Bogdanovich, Peter. "Josef von Sternberg." *Movie* 13 (Summer 1965).

Bond, Kirk. "Josef von Sternberg Revisited." *Film Courier,* Summer 1959.

———. "Joseph von Sternberg: Three Books." *Film Comment* 4, no. 2 (1967).

Bowers, Ronald L. "Marlene Dietrich, '54–'70." *Films in Review* 22, no. 1 (January 1971).

Brightman, Carol. "Midwest Film Festival." *Film Culture,* n.d.

Brownlow, Kevin. "Sternberg." *Film* 45 (Spring 1966).

Calendo, J. "Dietrich and the Devil." *Inter/View* 26 (October 1972).

———. "Dietrich and the Devil." *Inter/View* 27 (November 1972).

Combs, R. "The Salvation Hunters." *Monthly Film Bulletin* 45, no. 533 (June 1978).

"The Devil Is A Woman." *Classic Film Collector* 44 (Fall 1974).

Douchet, Jean. "Sternberg." *Cahiers du Cinema* 137 (November 1962).

E. E. B. "The Luck of von Sternberg." *Picture Goer* (London), January 1975.

"The Epic That Never Was." *Filmmakers Newsletter* 9, no. 4 (February 1976).

Esnault, Philippe, and Michele Firk. "Entretien avec Josef von Sternberg." *Positif* (Paris) 37–38 (January–March 1961).

"Films from the Archive." *(Underworld.)* Museum of Modern Art Pamphlet, available for study at Museum of Modern Art Film Study Center, n.d.

Firda, Richard Allen. "Literary Origins: Sternberg's Film: *The Blue Angel.*" *Literature/Film Quarterly* 7, no. 2 (1979).

Flinn, Tom. "Joe, Where Are You?" *The Velvet Light Trap* 17 (Winter 1977).

———. "The Scarlet Empress." *The Velvet Light Trap* 16 (Fall 1976).

Florey, Robert. "Escape." *(The Exquisite Sinner) Cinemonde* (Paris) 7 February 1949.

———. "Ma carrière à Hollywood." *Hollywood, d'hier, et d'aujourd'hui.* Paris: Edition Prisma, 1948.

Fox, J. "Cult Movies: *Blonde Venus.*" *Films and Filming* 23, no. 12 (September 1977).

Geoghegan, S. "Anatahan." *Film News* 32 (November–December 1975).

Gibbons, M. "Sternberg." *Film Mercury,* 2 January 1931.

Gow, Gordon. "Cult Movies: *Shanghai Gesture*." *Films and Filming* 24, no. 8 (May 1978).

———. "Alchemy: Dietrich and Sternberg." *Films and Filming* 20 (June 1974).

Graves, Charles. "Celebrities in Cameo, no. 50—Josef von Sternberg." *The Bystander* (London), 9 December 1936.

"Great Moments from *Morocco*." *Cinema Papers*, December 1974 (frame stills).

Green, O. O. "Six Films of Josef von Sternberg." *Movie* 13 (Summer 1965).

Griffith, Richard. "A Petty Bourgeois Tart Revived." *Saturday Review*, 2 December 1950.

———. "Marlene Dietrich: Image and Legend." Museum of Modern Art Film Library. 1959.

Harrington, Curtis. "Arrogant Gesture." *Theatre Arts* 34 (November 1950).

———. "The Most Dangerous Compromise." *The Hollywood Quarterly* 3, no. 4 (1949).

———. "An Index to the Films of Josef von Sternberg." Edited by Herman Weinberg. Index Series, 17. *The British Film Institute*, February 1949.

———. "Joseph von Sternberg." *Cahiers du Cinema*, October–November 1951.

Hervey, Harry. *Shanghai Express*. Treatment available for study at the Film Study Center, Museum of Modern Art, New York.

Higham, Charles. "Dietrich in Sydney." *Sight and Sound* 35 (Winter 1965–66).

Hollander, Anne. "The Gatsby Look and Other Costume Movie Blunders." *New York* 7, no. 21 (27 May 1974).

"Hollywood and von Sternberg." *The New York Post* 26 (January 1956).

Howard, Ron. "The Sternberg Gesture—Symbolism and Imagery in His Films." *Film Digest*, September 1967.

Jacobs, Lea. "The Censorship of *Blonde Venus:* Textual Analysis and Historical Methods." *Cinema Journal* 27, no. 3 (Spring 1988).

Jameson, R. T. "Savoir-être *Morocco*." *Movietone News* 37 (November 1974).

"Jet Pilot." Review of *Jet Pilot*. *Films and Filming* 331 (April 1982).

Johnston, Claire. "Women's Cinema as Counter Cinema." *Notes on Women's Cinema*. London: Society for Education in Film and Television (1973).

Kliman, B. "An American Tragedy: Novel, Scenario and Films." *Literature/Film Quarterly* 3 (Summer 1977).

Knight, Arthur. "Marlene Dietrich." *Films in Review* 5 (December 1954).

Kracauer, Siegfried. "Critical Note on Josef von Sternberg." Fiche. Available for study at the Film Study Center, Museum of Modern Art, New York.

Krutnik, Frank. *"The Shanghai Gesture:* The Exotic and Melodrama." *Wide Angle* 4, no. 2 (1980).

Luft, Herbert G. "Erich Pommer, Part II." *Films in Review*, November 1959.

———. "Josef von Sternberg—A Study." *Film Journal* (Melbourne) 24 (December 1964).

———. "Josef von Sternberg, Impressions and Remembrances." *Films in Review* 32, no. 1 (January 1981).

———. "Josef von Sternberg." *Filmkunst* (Vienna) 45 (1966).

Mackenzie, A. "Leonardo of the Lenses." *Life and Letters Today*, Spring 1936.

Macklin, F. A. "Interview with Josef von Sternberg." *Film Heritage,* Winter 1965–66.

"The Man Who Knows 20,000,000 Minds." *Hong Kong Daily Press,* 19 September 1936.

Milne, Tom. "An American Tragedy." *Monthly Film Bulletin* 42 (December 1975)

———. "Dishonored." *Monthly Film Bulletin* 45, no. 531 (April 1978).

———. "Thunderbolt." *Monthly Film Bulletin* 41, no. 487 (August 1974).

"A Native Returns." *The New York Times,* 10 September 1950.

Nugent, John. "The Puppeteer." *Newsweek,* 29 March 1965.

Ortoni, William. "Hollywood Has Nothing to Learn." *Atlantic Monthly,* June 1931.

Pankake, John. "Sternberg at 70." *Films in Review,* May 1964.

Potamkin, H. A. "Field Generals of the Film." *Vanity Fair,* March 1932.

Pringle, Henry F. "All for Art." *The New Yorker* 28 (March 1931).

Pulleine, T. "The Scarlet Empress." *Monthly Film Bulletin* 45, no. 533 (June 1978).

Rankin, Ruth. "Undraping Hollywood." *Photoplay* 45, no. 3 (February 1934).

Regan, Robert. "Dietrich and von Sternberg." *Moviescope* 1, no. 4, n.d.

Reisch, Walter. "Josef von Sternberg." *Action* 5, no. 1 (January–February 1970).

Rheuben, Joyce. "Josef von Sternberg: The Scientist and the Vamp." *Sight and Sound* 42, no. 1 (1972–73).

Rosenbaum, Jonathan. "Sternberg's Sayonara Gesture." *Film Comment* 14, no. 1 (January–February 1978).

Russell, Lee. "Josef von Sternberg." *New Left Review* 36 (March–April 1966).

"The Salvation Hunters." *The Director,* December 1924.

Sargeant, Winthrop. "Dietrich and Her Magic Myth." *Life 33,* 18 August 1952.

"The Scarlet Empress." Review of *The Scarlet Empress.* London *Times,* 10 May 1934.

Seaman, Ann Rowe. *Cinema Texas: Program Notes* 9, no. 2 (7 October 1975).

Sennwald, André. *"Catherine the Great."* Review of "Catherine the Great. The New York Times, 15 February 1934.

———. *"The Scarlet Empress."* Review of *The Scarlet Empress. The New York Times,* 15 September 1934.

———, "Josef von Sternberg—Stylist." *The New York Times,* 23 September 1934.

Shafer, Rosalind. "Catherine To Be More Colorful Than Authentic." *Daily News,* 19 November 1933.

Sherwood, Robert E. "Shanghai Express." *Hollywood Spectator,* March 1932.

Silver, Charles. "Sternberg: In Memoriam." *The Village Voice,* 8 January 1970.

Smith, Jack. "Belated Appreciation of von Sternberg." *Film Culture* 31 (1963–64).

"Some Memorable Films" *(Underworld).* Museum of Modern Art pamphlet, available for study at MOMA Film Study Center, New York.

Sorel, E. "Movie Classics: *The Blue Angel.*" *Esquire* 93 (April 1980).

Stein, Elliott. "Fun in a Chinese Laundry." *Sight and Sound,* Autumn 1965.

Thayer, J. E. "American Tragedy Original." *Classic Film Collector* 52 (Fall 1976).

Tibbetts, J. "Sternberg and *The Last Command.*" *Cinema Journal* 15, no. 2 (Spring 1976).

Tully, Jim. "Josef von Sternberg." *Vanity Fair,* July 1928.

Watts, Richard, Jr. *"Catherine the Great."* Review of *Catherine the Great. New York Herald Tribune,* 15 February 1934.

———. *"The Scarlet Empress."* Review of *The Scarlet Empress. New York Herald Tribune,* 15 September 1934.

Weinberg, Herman. "Director's Return." *The New York Times,* 6 November 1949.

———. "Fun in a Chinese Laundry." *The Village Voice,* 29 July 1965.

———. "Has von Sternberg Discovered a Japanese Dietrich?" *Theatre Arts* 37, no. 8 (August 1953).

———. "The Lost Films." *Sight and Sound,* August 1962.

———. "Sternberg and Stroheim." *Sight and Sound* (Winter 1965–66).

Weisstein, U. "Professor Unrat and the Blue Angel: Translations and Adaptations of Heinrich Mann's Novel in Two Media." *Film Journal* 1, nos. 3–4 (Fall–Winter 1972).

Whitehall, Richard. "Dietrich and *The Blue Angel." Films and Filming* 9, no. 1 (October 1962).

Willis, D. "Sternberg: The Context of Passion." *Sight and Sound* 47, no. 2 (Spring 1978).

Wood, Robin. "Venus de Marlene." *Film Comment* 14, no. 2 (March–April 1978).

Zucker, Carole. "Some Observations on Sternberg and Dietrich." *Cinema Journal* 19, no. 2 (Spring 1980).

Sternberg in Larger Works: Studies Containing Significant Information on Sternberg

Baxter, John. *Hollywood in the 'Thirties.* New York: Warner, 1970.

Bowser, Eileen, ed. *Film Notes.* New York: Museum of Modern Art, 1969.

Braudy, Leo. *The World in a Frame.* New York: Anchor, 1977.

Brownlow, Kevin. *The Parade's Gone By.* New York: Alfred A. Knopf, 1968.

Cameron, Ian. *Movie Reader.* New York: Praeger, 1972.

Casty, Alan. *Development of Film.* New York: Harcourt, Brace, 1963.

Conger, Syndy, and Janice Welsch, eds. *Narrative Strategies: Original Essays in Film and Prose Fiction.* Western Illinois Press, 1980.

Cook, David. *A History of Narrative Film.* New York: W. W. Norton, 1981.

Corliss, Richard, ed. *The Hollywood Screenwriters.* New York: Avon, 1972.

Dickens, Homer. *The Films of Marlene Dietrich.* New York: Citadel, 1968.

Dyer, Richard, ed. *Gays and Film.* London: British Film Institute, 1977.

———. *Stars.* London: British Film Institute, 1979.

Frewin, Leslie. *Dietrich.* New York: Avon, 1967.

Hardy, Forsyth, ed. *Grierson on Documentary.* New York: Harcourt, Brace, 1947.

Haskell, Molly. *From Reverence to Rape.* New York: Holt, Rinehart and Winston, 1973.

Higham, Charles. *Marlene.* New York: W. W. Norton, 1977.

Jacobs, Lewis. *The Rise of the American Film.* New York: Columbia UP, 1968.

Kaplan, E. Ann. *Women and Film*. New York: Methuen, 1983.

Kay, Karyn, and Gerald Peary, eds. *Women and the Cinema*. New York: E. P. Dutton, 1977.

Kobal, John. *Dietrich*. New York: E. P. Dutton, 1968.

Korda, Michael. *Charmed Lives*. New York: Avon, 1979.

Kracauer, Siegfried. *From Caligari to Hitler*. Princeton: Princeton UP, 1947.

MacDonald, Dwight. *On Movies*. New York: Berkeley, 1969.

Manvell, Roger. *Love Goddesses of the Movies*. New York: Hamlyn, 1975.

McConnell, Frank. *The Spoken Seen*. Baltimore: Johns Hopkins UP, 1975.

Mordden, Ethan. *Movie Stars*. New York: St. Martin's, 1983.

Morley, Sheridan. *Marlene Dietrich*. New York: McGraw-Hill, 1976.

Nichols, Bill. *Ideology and the Image*. Bloomington: Indiana UP, 1981.

Rideout, Eric. *The American Film*. London: Mitre, 1937.

Ross, T. J. *Film and the Liberal Arts*. New York: Holt, Rinehart and Winston, 1970.

Sarris, Andrew. *The American Cinema*. New York: E. P. Dutton, 1968.

———, ed. *Interviews with Film Directors*. New York: Avon, 1967.

Silver, Charles. *Marlene Dietrich*. New York: Pyramid, 1974.

Sontag, Susan. *Against Interpretation*. New York: Dell, 1966.

Spoto, Donald. *Falling in Love Again*. Boston: Little, Brown, 1985.

Walker, Alexander. *The Celluloid Sacrifice*. New York: Hawthorn, 1967.

Wollen, Peter. *Signs and Meaning in the Cinema*. Bloomington: Indiana UP, 1969.

Wood, Robin. *Personal Views*. London: Gordon Fraser, 1976.

Monographic Works on Sternberg

Baxter, John. *The Cinema of Josef von Sternberg*. New York: A. S. Barnes, 1971.

Baxter, Peter, ed. *Sternberg*. London: British Film Institute, 1980.

DelGaudio, Sybil. "Clothing Signification in the Films of Josef von Sternberg." Ph.D. diss., Columbia University, 1986.

The Filmcritic, Tokyo. "Josef von Sternberg." The entire issue of 108 pages is devoted to a critical study of Sternberg's work.

Goetz, Alice, Helmut Banz, and Otto Kellner, eds. *Josef von Sternberg, Eine Darstellung*. Published by the Society of German Film Clubs on the occasion of the Sternberg retrospective at Mannheim Internationale Filmwoche, 1966.

Kinematek. "Josef von Sternberg." October, 1967. The entire issue is devoted to a study of his life and work.

Milgrom, Al, ed. *The Cinema of Josef von Sternberg: A Compendium of Critical Commentary, Opinion and Historical Notes on Sternberg and his Work*. University Film Society, University of Minnesota, 1964.

Positif 75 (May 1966). "Marlene Dietrich and Josef von Sternberg." Special issue.

Studlar, Gaylyn. *In the Realm of Pleasure: Von Sternberg, Dietrich and the Masochistic Aesthetic*. Urbana and Chicago: University of Illinois, 1988.

Sarris, Andrew. *The Films of Josef von Sternberg*. New York: Museum of Modern Art, 1966.

Weinberg, Herman. *Josef von Sternberg*. New York: E. P. Dutton, 1967.

Zucker, Carole. *The Idea of the Image*. London and Toronto: Associated University Presses, 1988.

Works by Sternberg

Sternberg, Josef von. "Acting in Film and Theatre." *Film Culture* 5–6 (Winter 1955).

———. *The Blue Angel* (authorized translation of German continuity). New York: Simon and Schuster, 1968.

———. "Come studio i mei film." *Cinema* (Rome) 3 (1936).

———. "Créer avec l'oeil." *L'Art du cinema* par Pierre Lherminier. Paris: Editions Seghers, 1960.

———. "Del estetismo a la filosofia." *Gaceto del festival Mar del plata*, 21 March 1963.

———. *Fun in a Chinese Laundry*. New York: Collier, 1965.

———. *Daughters of Vienna*. Vienna, 1922. Trans. from the German of Karl Adolph.

———. "Le Jeu au theatre et au cinema." *Cahiers du cinema*. Paris: Noel, 1956.

———. "More Light." *Sight and Sound* 25 (Fall 1955).

———. *Morocco and Shanghai Express* (scripts). New York: Simon and Schuster, 1973.

———. "On Life and Film." *Films in Review* 3, no. 8 (October 1952).

———. "A Taste for Celluloid." *Films and Filming*, July 1963.

———. "The von Sternberg Principle." *Esquire*, October 1963.

———. "The Waxen Galatea." *The Director*. Hollywood, 1925 (short story).

Costume

Anderson, S. H. "Fifty Years' Glamour in Film Fashions." *The New York Times*, 8 September 1980.

Anger, Kenneth. *Hollywood Babylon*. San Francisco: Straight Arrow, 1975.

Bailey, Margaret. *Those Glorious, Glamour Years*. Secaucus, N.J.: Citadel, 1982.

Banton, Travis. "Fashions for the Stars." *Motion Picture Studio Insider* 1, no. 1 (May 1935).

Barthes, Roland. *Critical Essays*, trans. Richard Howard. Evanston: Northwestern UP, 1972.

———. *The Fashion System*, trans. Matthew Ward and Richard Howard. Toronto: McGraw-Hill, 1983.

———. *Mythologies*. New York: Hill and Wang, 1957.

Batterberry, Michael and Ariane. *Mirror, Mirror: A Social History of Fashion*. New York: Holt, Rinehart and Winston, 1977.

Bell, Arthur. "Toot, Toot, Tootsie Hello." *The Village Voice*, 28 December 1982.

Bell-Metereau, Rebecca. *Hollywood Androgyny*. New York: Columbia UP, 1985.

Bihalji-Merin. *Great Masks.* New York: Harry N. Abrams, 1970.

Bogatyrev, Peter. "Costume as a Sign (The Functional and Structural Concept of Costume in Ethnography)." In *Semiotics of Art,* ed. Ladislav Matejka and Irwin Titunik. Cambridge: M.I.T. Press, 1977.

Cantwell, Mary. "Sexual Masquerade is Conveying A New Kind of Message." *The New York Times,* 16 January 1983.

Carr, Larry. *Four Fabulous Faces.* New Rochelle, N.Y.: Arlington House, 1970.

Carter, Ernestine. *The Changing World of Fashion.* New York: G. P. Putnam's, 1977.

Chase, Donald. "The Costume Designer." In *Filmmaking: The Collaborative Art.* Boston: Little, Brown, 1975.

Chierichetti, David. *Hollywood Costume Design.* New York: Harmony Books, 1976.

Cooper, Wendy. *Hair.* New York: Stein and Day, 1971.

Davidson, D. "From Virgin to Dynamo: The Amoral Woman in European Cinema." *Cinema Journal* 21, no. 1 (1981).

Doane, Mary Ann. "Woman's Stake: Filming the Female Body." *October* 17 (Summer 1981).

"Does Hollywood Create?" *Vogue* 81, no. 3 (1 February 1933).

Duka, John. "The Conservative Tradition." *The New York Times Magazine,* 27 March 1983.

Eckert, Charles. "The Carole Lombard in Macy's Window." *Quarterly Review of Film Studies,* Winter 1970.

Ewen, Stuart and Elizabeth. *Channels of Desire.* New York: McGraw-Hill, 1982.

Field, Alice Evans. "Costume Design." In *Hollywood U.S.A. From Script to Screen.* New York: Vantage, 1952.

Flugel, J. C. *The Psychology of Clothes.* New York: International Universities, 1930.

Forbes, Pamela Pratt. "The Men Behind the Gowns." *Cinema Arts* 1, no. 1 (June 1937).

Fraser, Kennedy. *The Fashionable Mind.* New York: Alfred A. Knopf, 1981.

Gaines, Jane. "The Queen Christina Tie-Ups: Convergence of Show Window and Screen." *Quarterly Review of Film and Video* 2, no. 1 (1989).

Gaines, Jane, and Herzog, Charlotte. *Fabrications.* New York: Routledge, 1990.

———. "Hildy Johnson and the 'Man-Tailored Suit': The Comedy of Inequality." *Film Reader 5* (1982).

Gaines, William. "Hollywood Snubs Paris." *Photoplay* 46, no. 5 (April 1934).

Gilbert, Sandra. "Costumes of the Mind: Transvestism as Metaphor in Modern Literature." *Critical Inquiry* 7, no. 2 (Winter 1980).

Gorsline, Douglas. *What People Wore.* New York: Viking, 1952.

Gubar, Susan. "Blessings in Disguise: Cross Dressing as Re-Dressing for Female Modernists." *Massachusetts Review,* Autumn 1981.

Gurel, Lois and Marianne Beeson. *Dimensions of Dress and Adornment.* Dubuque: Kendall/Hunt, 1975.

Head, Edith, and Paddy Calistro. *Edith Head's Hollywood.* New York: E. P. Dutton, 1983.

Henley, Nancy. *Body Politics.* Englewood Cliffs, N.J.: Prentice-Hall, 1977.

Hollander, Anne. "The Gatsby Look and Other Costume Movie Blunders." *New York* 7, no. 21 (27 May 1974).

———. *Seeing Through Clothes*. New York: Avon, 1980.

Konig, René. *The Restless Image*. London: George Allen and Unwin, 1973.

Langner, Lawrence. *The Importance of Wearing Clothes*. New York: Hastings House, 1959.

Lauer, Robert, and Jeanette Lauer. *Fashion Power*. Englewood Cliffs, N.J.: Prentice-Hall, 1981.

Laver, James. *Modesty in Dress*. Boston: Houghton Mifflin, 1969.

LaVine, Robert. *In A Glamourous Fashion*. New York: Charles Scribner's, 1980.

Leese, Elizabeth. *Costume Design in the Movies*. New York: Frederick Ungar, 1977.

Lester, K. M. and B. V. Oerke. *Accessories of Dress*. Peoria, Ill.: Manual Arts, 1940.

Lurie, Alison. *The Language of Clothes*. New York: Random House, 1981.

McConathy, Dale, and Diana Vreeland. *Hollywood Costume: Glamour! Glitter! Romance!* New York: Harry N. Abrams, 1976.

Rosen, Marjorie. "Movie Costumes." *Film Comment* 11, no. 2 (March–April 1975).

Stephenson, Ralph, and J. R. Debrix. "Costume." In *The Cinema As Art*. Baltimore: Penguin, 1965.

Thorpe, Margaret Farrand. "Cinema Fashions." In *America at the Movies*. New Haven: Yale UP, 1939.

Turim, Maureen. "Gentlemen Consume Blondes." *Wide Angle* 1, no. 1 (1979).

Wilcox, Ruth Turner. *The Mode in Costume*. New York: Scribner's, 1949.

Yarwood, Doreen. *The Encyclopedia of World Costume*. New York: Scribner's, 1978.

Other Works Cited

Arnheim, Rudolf. *Film As Art*. Berkeley: University of California, 1967.

Bade, Patrick. *Femme Fatale*. New York: Mayflower, 1979.

Barsacq, Leon. *Caligari's Cabinet and Other Grand Illusions*. Boston: New York Graphic Society, 1970.

Bazin, André. *What Is Cinema?* Trans. Hugh Gray. Berkeley: University of California, 1972.

Heilbrun, Carolyn. *Toward a Recognition of Androgyny*. New York: W. W. Norton, 1973.

Johnston, Claire. "Femininity and the Masquerade: *Anne of the Indies*." In *Jacques Tourneur*, ed. Claire Johnston and Paul Willeman. Edinburgh: Edinburgh Film Festival, 1975.

Kracauer, Siegfried. *Theory of Film*. New York: Oxford UP, 1960.

Lotman, Jurij. *Semiotics of Cinema*, trans. Mark E. Suino. Ann Arbor: University of Michigan, 1981.

Mitchell, Juliet, and Jacqueline Rose, eds. *Feminine Sexuality: Jacques Lacan and the "école freudienne."* New York: W. W. Norton, 1982.

Mulvey, Laura. "Visual Pleasure and Narrative Cinema." In *Women and the Cinema*, ed. Karyn Kay and Gerald Peary. New York: E. P. Dutton, 1977.

Riviere, Joan. "Womanliness as Masquerade." In *Psychoanalysis and Female Sexuality,* ed. Hendrik Ruitenbeek. New Haven, Conn.: College and UP Services, 1962.

Roberts-Jones, Phillipe. *Beyond Time and Place: Non-Realist Painting in the Nineteenth Century.* London: Oxford UP, 1978.

Russo, Vito. *The Celluloid Closet.* New York: Harper and Row, 1981.

Sharff, Stefan. *The Elements of Cinema.* New York: Columbia UP, 1982.

Troyat, Henri. *Catherine the Great.* New York: E. P. Dutton, 1980.

Tyler, Parker. *Screening the Sexes.* Toronto: Holt, Rinehart and Winston, 1972.

Zeitlin, Froma. "Travesties of Gender and Genre in Aristophanes' *Thesmophoriazousae.*" *Critical Inquiry* 8, no. 2 (Winter 1981).

Index

Agel, Henri, 119
Ager, Cecelia, 120
American Tragedy, An, 20, 76, 77
Anatahan, 15, 20, 21, 22, 97, 149, 156, 160, 166–70. See also *Saga of Anatahan, The*
Armstrong, John, 148
Arnheim, Rudolf, 18
Atwill, Lionel, 115
Audibert, Louis, 152

Babuscio, Jack, 99, 100, 104
Bailey, Margaret, 13, 16, 106
Balbusch, Peter, 130
Ballard, Lucien, 114
Bancroft, George, 25
Banton, Travis, 15, 16, 27, 56, 67, 75, 84, 114, 120, 123, 125, 128, 131, 132, 140, 142
Bara, Theda, 118
Barthes, Roland, 14, 50–51
Baudelaire, Pierre, 118–19
Baxter, John, 15, 27, 32, 68, 83, 87, 91, 115, 125, 129, 149
Baxter, Peter, 25, 38
Bazin, Andre, 18, 99
BBC, the, 148
Beale, Patrick, 118
Beery, Wallace, 66
Bell-Metereau, Rebecca, 60, 107
Belton, John, 81
Bendix, William, 156, 157
Bergner, Elisabeth, 130
Bihalji-Merin, Oto, 68–69
Birth of A Nation, The, 134
Blonde Venus, 21, 29, 32, 35, 39, 42–62, 68, 69, 73, 74, 94, 97, 101, 102, 108, 111, 113, 127, 143–45, 156
Blue Angel, The, 16, 21, 29–39, 42, 43, 53, 64, 69, 97, 101, 102, 124, 156
Bogdanovich, Peter, 93

Borzage, Frank, 81
Bow, Clara, 16
Bowser, Eileen, 28, 163
Braudy, Leo, 73, 135–36
Brent, Evelyn, 25, 27, 163
Brook, Clive, 25, 111
Brownlow, Kevin, 166

Cages, 118
Cahiers critics, 110
Caligula, 146
Caprice Espagnol (The Devil Is A Woman), 114
Carmen (Prosper Merimee), 119
Carmen (Georges Bizet), 119
Carnival, 27, 28, 90, 116, 153. *See also* Festival
Case of Lena Smith, The, 19
Cassini, Oleg, 153
Casty, Alan, 37
Catherine the Great (original title for *The Scarlet Empress*), 130
Catherine the Great (Paul Czinner film), 130–31, 148
Chierichetti, David, 13, 16, 75, 123, 140
Cinematheque Francaise, 135
City, the (as cinema), 149–58
Cocteau, Jean, 119
Colbert, Claudette, 16
Colton, John, 149
Columbia Pictures, 89–90, 146
Connolly, Walter, 90
Cooper, Gary, 102
Costume (as element of mise-en-scene): 14–15
Costume, Hollywood: and Travis Banton, 16–18; as element of directional style, 14–15; Barthes on, 14; previous works on, 13–14; signification, 14; Sternberg's interest in, 14–15; use in Dietrich cycle, 15

Costume signification: ambiguity, 151; ambivalent clothing, 36; androgyny, 36, 59–62, 101, 104, 107, 145, 151, 153; birds, 27; black, 82–83; blondness, 78; camp, 99–114; change, 79–80; concealment, 47, 77–78, 100, 118; cross-dressing, 59–62, 94, 101, 104, 107–8, 143–45; deception, 63–97, 149, 151, 158; disguise, 34, 50, 60–61, 63–97, 100, 104, 116, 118, 149, 151, 152, 156, 158; display, 34, 44; dressing, 35, 44, 50; dressing room, 48; dressing tables, 165; duality, 46; environmental costumes, 168; eroticism, 35–37, 46–47, 53, 57, 64, 106, 120, 136–37; exhibitionism, 44; exoticism, 39, 77, 86–87, 101, 118, 149, 150–51, 153, 156–58; feathers, 25, 27, 28; fur, 54, 64, 89, 140; glamour, 25, 57, 82, 118, 123–25; gloves, 89; greatcoat, 163–64; hats, 78, 111–12; history (*see also* period), 127–48; incongruity, 100–102, 110, 113; inaccessibility, 32, 39; lace, 82; layering, 32, 73–74, 96; Lesbianism, 54, 58–59; masks, 54–56, 68–69, 83, 116, 152–53; masquerade, 27, 60–62, 67–68, 70, 73, 116, 152–53; nudity, 42–45, 46–47, 50–51; paniers 34, 132, 137; patterns (fabric), 91; performance, 33–34, 42, 44; period (*see also* history), 90–91, 127–48; "problematic fit," 72–73; revelation, 50; role-playing, 47, 69, 72–73; "Russianization," 140, 143, 145; sequins, 82; sexual masquerade, 94, 104, 107–8, 143–45, 149; slacks, 106–7; spectacle, 77–78; spying, 63–97; striptease, 50–52, 94–96, 97; stylization, 99–125; undergarments, 35, 64; undressing, 35, 50, 73; uniforms, 66, 69, 70, 74–75, 76, 85, 91, 96, 101, 109, 119; veils, 78, 87–89; 102, 112, 118; Watteau style, 132, 137

Crime and Punishment, 20, 89
Crowther, Bosley, 150
Czinner, Paul, 130, 135, 148

de Beauvoir, Simone, 107
Devil Is A Woman, The, 15, 21, 22, 27, 32, 68, 99, 114–25, 135, 139, 156, 167
Dexter, Brad, 156

Dietrich, Marlene, 15, 16, 18, 20, 24, 27, 28, 30, 31, 33, 36, 37, 38, 39, 42, 43, 44, 45, 46, 48, 50, 51, 56, 57, 58, 63, 65, 66, 67, 68, 69–70, 72, 73, 75, 76, 77, 78, 84, 87, 89, 99, 101, 104, 106, 107, 108, 113, 114, 115, 118, 120, 121, 123, 124, 125, 128, 129, 132, 135, 136, 137, 139, 146, 149, 150, 151, 158, 167
Dietrich, Marlene (roles in Sternberg films): Amy Jolly *(Morocco)*, 102–25; Catherine the Great/Princess Sophia *(The Scarlet Empress)*, 127–46; Concha Perez *(The Devil Is A Woman)*, 115–25; Helen Faraday *(Blonde Venus)*, 42–62, Lola-Lola *(The Blue Angel)*, 29–39; Shanghai Lily *(Shanghai Express)*, 77–89, 157; "X-27" *(Dishonored)*, 63–77
Dionysus, 59
Dishonored, 21, 22, 27, 43, 53, 60, 63–77, 84, 89, 90, 91, 94, 96, 101, 116, 118, 151, 152, 156, 158
Docks of New York, The, 19, 20, 167
Dos Passos, John, 115
Drag Net, The, 16
Dreier, Hans, 129–30, 132
Dressmaker from Paris, The, 16
Dryden, Ernest, 90
Durgnat, Raymond (O. O. Green), 72, 73, 101, 153
Dyer, Richard, 72, 73

Eckert, Charles, 13
Eisenstein, Sergei, 135
Epic That Never Was, The, 148
Eve, 118
Exquisite, Sinner, The, 19

Fairbanks, Douglas, 69, 130
"Falling in Love Again" (song in *The Blue Angel*), 35–36, 39
Femme fatale, 78, 85, 118, 120, 153
Festival, 28, 90, 116, 153. *See also* Carnival
Fetish, 34, 35, 51, 61, 64, 104, 108
Fetishistic scopophilia, 108
Flinn, Tom, 134–35
"Flogging Block, The" (Swinburne poem), 119
Flugel, J. C., 36

Foreign Legion, 101–2
Furthman, Jules, 93, 149

Gaines, Jane, 13
Gaines, William, 128–29, 132
Garbo, Greta, 87
Garmes, Lee, 18, 77, 102
Grahame, Gloria, 158
Grant, Cary, 53
Graves, Robert, 146
Greer, Howard, 16
Griffith, D. W., 118, 134
Gubar, Susan, 59, 107
Guinness, Alec, 73

Harlow, Jean, 78
Haskell, Molly, 85
Hays Office, 42, 149
Head, Edith, 15, 27
Hecht, Ben, 25
Heilbrun, Carolyn, 59
Helen of Troy, 42
Herczeg, Geza, 149
Hitchcock, Alfred, 78
Hollander, Anne, 34, 82–83, 128, 131
Hollywood (as metaphor), 160–61, 163,
    164, 165
Honor, code of, 70, 76, 96, 119
Horton, Edward Everett, 116
"Hot Voodoo" (song in *Blonde Venus*),
    50, 51–53
Hughes, Howard, 93, 156
Huston, Walter, 150

I, Claudius, 15, 21, 22, 109, 146–48
Ivan Grozhny (Ivan the Terrible), 135
Ivanov, V. V., 18

Jannings, Emil, 30, 160
Jet Pilot, 20, 21, 22, 60, 66, 77, 89, 91–
    97, 109, 156, 158
Johnston, Claire, 61, 107
Jory, Victor, 90

Kaplan, E. Ann, 57
King Steps Out, The, 20, 22, 60, 66, 77,
    89–91
Knight Without Armor, 146
Kobal, John, 115, 119
Kollorsz, Richard, 130
Korda, Alexander, 130, 146

Korda, Michael, 146
Kracauer, Siegfried, 18
Krutnik, Frank, 150

Lacan, Jacques, 110
Lang, Fritz, 115
Langlois, Henri, 135
Langner, Lawrence, 36
Last Command, The, 19, 22, 24, 66, 73,
    160–66, 168, 170
Last Laugh, The, 163
Laughton, Charles, 146
LaVine, Robert, 13
Leese, Elizabeth, 13
Legs (Dietrich's), 37, 38, 64, 106
Leigh, Janet, 93, 97
Life magazine, 166
Lombard, Carole, 16, 78
Lotman, Jurij, 18–19, 29
Louys, Pierre, 115
Lubitsch, Ernst, 14, 16, 96, 114, 125,
    134
Lurie, Alison, 84

Macao, 20, 21, 22, 93, 102, 156–58, 167
Mann, Heinrich, 29, 32, 37
Marshall, Herbert, 42, 111
Maruyama, Michiro, 166
Mary Magdalene, 79
Mata Hari, 93
Mature, Victor, 149, 150, 153, 156
Mazurky, Mike, 152
McConathy, Dale, 13, 123
McConnell, Frank, 32
McLaglen, Victor, 63
Menjou, Adolphe, 24, 102
Military code, 69, 85, 86
Mirrors, 163, 164
Miscegenation, 151
Mitchum, Robert, 156, 158
Mordden, Ethan, 69
Moore, Grace, 90
Morocco, 15, 21, 22, 32, 35, 39, 58, 64,
    66, 69, 77, 84, 94, 97, 99–114, 115,
    124, 143–45, 156
Moullet, Luc, 97
Mukarovsky, Jan, 18
Mulvey, Laura, 107, 110
Munson, Ona, 150, 152
Murnau, F. W., 161, 163

Negishi, Akemi, 166
Nets, 23, 82, 116, 118
Nichols, Bill, 50, 53, 108
Ninotchka, 96

Oberon, Merle, 146
Oland, Warner, 63
Oms, Marcel, 28, 90, 152
Ophuls, Max, 14
Orphee (Cocteau), 119

Pabst, G. W., 135
Paramount, 15–18, 106, 114, 115, 124, 125, 129
Patriot, The, 134
Peter of Russia (Peter the Great), 136, 142
Pickford, Mary, 16
Plunkett, Walter, 128
Pompadour, Madame, 132, 143
Powell, William, 24, 160
Preminger, Otto, 14
Pressburger, Arnold, 149
Professor Unrat (Heinrich Mann novel), 29
Prostitute/streetwalker/prostitution, 65, 75

Ray, Nicholas, 156
Rheuben, Joyce, 19, 69, 78, 139, 145
Rise of Louis XIV, The, 136
Rittau, Gunter, 33
Riviere, Joan, 109–10
RKO (studio), 93
Robson, Flora, 146
Romero, Cesar, 115
Rops, Felicien, 32
Rosenmeyer, Thomas, 59
Rosher, Charles, 33
Rossellini, Roberto, 29, 136
Russell, Jane, 156, 158

Sadomasochism, 119
Saga of Anatahan, The, 15, 20, 21, 22, 97, 149, 156, 166–70. See also *Anatahan*
Salome, 118
Salvation Hunters, The, 15, 16, 19, 21, 23–24, 153
Sarris, Andrew, 24, 32, 34, 36, 76, 90, 102, 115, 116, 120, 135, 153, 156, 157, 163, 170
Scarlet Empress, The, 21, 22, 23, 68, 90, 91, 97, 101, 116, 127–46, 153
Schulberg, B. P., 15, 114, 125
Sea Gull, The, 19
Self-reflexivity, 73, 160–70
Sennwald, Andre, 130, 131
Sergeant Madden, 20, 66
Seyffertitz, Gustav von, 65, 66
Shanghai Express, 21, 22, 39, 43, 53, 60, 64, 66, 70, 73, 77–89, 90, 91, 94, 108, 111, 118, 151, 152, 156, 157, 158, 167
Shanghai Gesture, The, 20, 21, 22, 89, 109, 149–56, 157, 158, 167
Shklovsky, Viktor, 18
Siebert, Maria, 136
Soldier, 70
Song of Songs, 87
Sontag, Susan, 100, 104
Sternberg, Josef von: apprenticeship in millinery shop, 15; association with Banton, Dietrich, and Paramount, 15–18; attention to costume as sign in his work, 14–15; character analogues, 23–24, 102, 104, 109, 114–15, 166; creation of Dietrich persona, 31–32; Dietrich cycle of films and costume signs, 20; exploration of cinematic essence, 18–20; films of (listed alphabetically in index); interest in clothing, 15; linking of beauty with danger, 53; position on the nuclear family, 47, 56–58; relationship to actors, 31; resistance to film's documentary tendency, 19–20, 25, 29, 99–100; struggles with the Hollywood system, 20
Stroheim, Erich von, 15, 25
Swan Lake, 78–79
Swinburne, Algernon Charles, 118–19
Sjostrom, Victor, 161
Stiller, Mauritz, 161

Thunderbolt, 19, 20
Tierney, Gene, 149, 150, 156
Tone, Franchot, 90
Toulouse-Lautrec, Henri, 37
Troyat, Henri, 142
Turim, Maureen, 13, 78
Tynyanov, Ju, 18

UFA (studio), 15, 129
Underworld, 19, 21, 23, 24, 25–28, 116

Vanity Fair (magazine), 101
Varady, 16
Virgin/whore dichotomy, 69
Vollmoller, Karl, 149
Vreeland, Diana, 13, 123

Walker, Alexander, 33, 69, 89
Walker, Dr. Mary, 59–60
Watts, Richard, Jr., 130, 131
Wayne, John, 94, 96

Weinberg, Herman, 101, 115, 124, 156, 167
Welles, Orson, 14, 89
West, Mae, 16, 78
Williams, Emlyn, 146
Wollen, Peter, 29, 86, 99
Woman and Puppet (The Devil Is A Woman), 115
Wong, Anna May, 78, 87
Wood, Robin, 46, 51, 53, 62, 137, 139, 146
Woulfe, Michael, 93
Wyler, William, 14

Zukor, Adolph, 106, 140